"Everybody's Got An ITCH"

CHAPTER 1

It is funny how life can sometimes throw an unexpected curve ball in your life. You are discombobulated and stressed. You are just straight pinned to the wall. Yes. You are attached to undetailed walls, that somewhat holds your future in its hands. These types of walls are labeled undetailed because it does not know for sure why you are put in a place or certain level of folk that sometimes just don't know what the hell they're talking about. It is crazy, deranged, pitiful, yet ridiculous.

The Bible says there is reason for everything and a season for all new changes. Well, if a change is something that person wants to do at that moment, then, act like the commercial "Nike", and just do it. So, rejoice in whatever goals, 5-day, to 5-year plan, and be glad. Weeping may endure for a night, but joy definitely comes in the morning. Well, joy finally came for this dark-skinned, girl named Rachel Simone Kelly. Rachel is originally from Brooklyn, New York.

Six years ago, when she was only 14 years-old, a terrible tragedy had struck Rachel's mother. Her mother used to be a drug addict. Her mother never used to be this way in the beginning of her precious lifetime.

Rachel's mother was 31 years-old and was light-skinned. Her frame was slim and petite and she too had those same chingy brown eyes that Rachel has now. Her mother had long thick black hair that dropped to her backside. All the men called her Ms. Red-bone bunny, because she was so fine and so light-skinned.

Rachel's father was a 36-year-old, dark-skinned brother. He did not finish junior high, but he tried to find work where ever he could to keep food on the table. He wore an afro, which was sometimes cut and sometimes raggedy. He stayed close to her mother, because she always held down a job, and had a better education than he did. He was very jealous and over protective of her mother.

Her mother was a registered nurse at one of Brooklyn's hospital. She worked a lot of over-time and made a lot of money. Yet, still, she never wanted to move out of the projects. As a child herself, right up to adulthood, her mother lived in the projects most of her life. Rachel's mother felt comfortable in her surroundings, because there were a lot of people around. She thought that was the life and it was nothing more outside of what she was already doing, living, and dreaming at that moment. Her mother had a steady boyfriend, after her and Rachel's father separated, and a sista-girl friend, named Debbie, who was on welfare and had four kids out of wedlock. Every man ran through Debbie like a bad case of diarrhea.

Rachel's mother never looked down on her friends and never tried to act better than them, even if she was more educated. Sometimes those degrees that a person holds can't always compare to the strong love and friendship that a person seeks in their time of need. Debbie was also a heroin addict and Rachel's mother used to try to tell her that if she did not slow down, that drug would kill her and her children would be taken into a terrible foster home. Or, even worse, probably end up on the streets and using drugs.

Debbie would always use the excuse that she was depressed and need a man in her life to ease the pain and fill a vacant hole in her life. Debbie had four kids. Now, if those kids did not fill enough holes to keep her happy, then she was pretty much out of luck. But, if a person had to look deeper, it would be a freaking' hot mess.

Sometimes a woman, who was of Debbie's character, could have possibly needed a father figure for herself as well, keeping her sane.

Rachel's father left her mother because he felt that she was too smart for him. Just because her mother wanted to further her education and be somebody in life, her father hated her mother to the fullest extreme.

Her father never made it passed the ninth grade, and his reading skills were on a third-grade level. Whenever he felt like her mother was getting ahead, he would try to kill her dream. When he got high off the bad heroin, he would come home and beat her mother to a pulp. Her mother used to have bruises so bad, that she could not even go to work.

Finally, her mother got tired of him beating on her and she went to a little hustler on the street corner, bought a semi-automatic gun and shot Rachel's father right in the ass. He has not been seen since. After a while, Rachel's mother began to miss him and started to withdraws.

Rachel's mother turned to heroin to make it through the day. Then it turned into an every week fix. This was an unusual change for her mother. Rachel did not know where and when this started. All she knew was that she wanted her mother's pain to stop. The money was getting slim and food was definitely not on the table every night like it used to be. Seven days a week, her mother shot up heroin like it was going out of style. They needed the bills to be paid and her mother did not go to work enough to collect a paycheck.

Their two-bedroom apartment started to feel like grand central station. She had so many different men running in and out of that little apartment, it was pitiful. Some of the men that came to the apartment were dressed clean and some were just straight up dirty. Some of the men tried to act pleasant and the other was just rude, obnoxious and sometimes abusive to her mother. Rachel could not understand why her mother had stooped to such a low in her young adult life. Her mother was beautiful, smart and well educated.

Late at night, Rachel could hear her mother crying in the bathroom. The water in the bathtub would be running and the door would always stay locked. That next night, Rachel quietly climbed out of bed and crawled on her hands and knees towards the squeaky bedroom door. She heard her mother arguing with a man in the living room. She slowly cracked the bedroom door open and saw her mother lying on the floor, in a crunched position. It was almost like a fetal position.

It was a very large husky man standing in the other room. He was slumped over her mother. His right fist was balled up so tight; it had single lines of blood flowing from it. His left hand had her mother's long black thick hair wrapped round his fist. He was all sweaty and breathing extremely heavy. He started to speak in a deep tone. He was reaping of alcohol.

"You listen to me and you listen to me good. I am not done with you yet. When I get done with digging in you, the way I want to dig in you then you can get up".

You could hear Rachel's mother sobbing softly, while she continued to lie on the cold floor. She was trying to plead this man to turn her loose.

"Please, my baby's sleep right in the next room. I don't want her to see me like this.

"Oh, is that right".

This man was a real pig of nature and he started to think the trashiest thing that only an inconsiderate human being would ever think of doing. That is only if there decent, and with morals.

"Well, since you can't stay down, then maybe I'll just get a fresh piece from baby girl in the next room".

"Please. I will do whatever you want. Please, just don't mess with my baby.

"Good. I thought would see it my way".

This man continued with his business and worked her mother over like a horse- trainer working a large stable of horses, for a major competition.

At times, Rachel wanted to ask her mother why she had let these men just run over her like a train running on its daily time schedule. Being that her mother was so care-free and did not want to hurt other people's feelings, she thought that her mother enjoyed the company of men at her door step. Seeing how not enough money was coming in the house from her mother's paycheck, some of the men that her mother dealt with actually left some money on the coffee table, when they got finished handling their business with her mother. Too bad it was not enough to pay the rent, bills, and groceries.

A year and a half later, her mother met another man. He was a lawyer. Sexy as all hell, and he had a height of 6'9 and weighed only 175 pounds. His name was Larry Tucker.

Larry was a very well-dressed man and extremely smart, except for one thing, he had a drug problem. He always said that he could control it, but he never could control his temper. He started beating on Rachel's mother too, and early. Her mother felt like this was as good as she was going to get. A fine, sexy lawyer, who is smart, yet a drug addict. (Wow).

She claimed that if he could keep it together, and at the same time, keep from whooping her ass, she would stay with him. Again, she never looked down on anybody and felt it was the right thing to do. Her mother chose to ignore his drug problem.

She loved this man and did not want to lose him. Every night her mother's boyfriend wanted to go out and get high after a hard day's work. Some days her mother tried to keep him in the house. He was the only man in her eyes that seemed to only rock her world.

She was stressed and wandered what she would do if she were to lose this man. She went out with him every night and started to get high. She did it because she did not want him to think that she was too good to party, the way he partied. One more thing, this sexy fine lawyer was married. He's separated, but still married.

Larry still lived in the other house with his wife. He told Rachel's mother that he was sleeping in separate rooms from his wife. He told her mother that if he tried to get a divorce, his wife would take everything he owned, including the red, sun-roof C 320 Mercedes Benz.

At that time, Rachel's mother did not have proper transportation. She used to take the subway trains, or if she ran extremely late, her mother would call for a cab. So seeing Larry in the Mercedes Benz was her mother's highlight of the day. In spite of everything that went on, she chose to deal with Larry's scandalous situation. Rachel's mother was an amateur, when it came to being with a man of his stature. Larry, of course, was a professional. A professional liar.

By the way, he handled his situations at home extremely well, and with her mother being the other woman, the mistress of the night, his personal flunky. He was good. He was very good. Her mother was so weak for a man, that she would almost do anything to keep them in her life. While she was trying to put her life back on track, Larry was coming out of the closet, getting more and more addicted to heroin. He knew how to hook lonely-desperate women, into his nasty, disgusting web. He dealt with women, who felt like this was the life, to be with this type of man. Crazy and deranged, is the word for this case of missing link relationships. **Crazy and deranged.**

Rachel's mother thought that this type of behavior was okay, as long as the man is pleased, and does not put his foot in your neck every now and then. She thought this was all done out of love. Well, it wasn't. It was done out of fear of being alone again. All of her mother's self-respect went flying right out of the apartment window.

Seeing how she loved this man so, so much, she allowed him to continue on with his unstable situation. **His Lies, abuse and terrible misuse**. After some time had passed, Rachel's mother started to grow tired and wanted her so-called man, to make a decision, and depart from his disturbing situation. This man used to coldly look at her, with flaming red eyes. He would remind her time and time again.... "You knew what it was when you started seeing me. Why are you changing now?" Rachel wondered if her mother met this man in her past life, before she met Rachel's father.

"I'm not changing, Larry, I just thought that you might want to be here instead of with your wife. I mean, you are always here. You're always trying to act as if I'm the only one for you".

"I act as I damn well please. If I want you every night, then I'm gonna' have you every night. Besides, you should have put your foot down and corrected my bad ass from the door.

"You are kidding, right? She says in a shaky voice, not knowing if Larry is going to swing to punch her, or throw his arms up to give her a great big hug. Picture that one…

"I'm not changing. You can either deal with it, or you can leave". More and more time went on, and she dealt with it, day in and day out. She committed to being humiliated more from this man, who she thought loved her, adored her, and cherished her.

As a young girl, Rachel endlessly watched her mother live life by trying to please a man who did not completely belong to her. This man deliberately tried to have his cake and a turkey dinner. Rachel's mother tried to change Larry, but he became more violent and continued to lose control of his temper. He began to beat on her mother, and she in turn lost her dignity, pride and self-esteem.

Her mother tried to hide her bruises from Rachel. Her mother would tell her that she fell, or walked into the wall, trying to find the light switch. Her mother was unable to shake her intense infatuation for this man. Her worldly lust for this man was unexplained. This man was sexy, 6 foot 10 inches tall. The complexion of his skin was dark brown. From his shoulder-blades right down to the calves was crafted just right, almost like connecting the dots.

Judging from the structure of this man, a person would have thought he was a professional ball player. Well, he was not a dark and sexy Denzel Washington or deep, dish of milk chocolate Morris Chestnut, but he was fine. Yet still, she felt for this man, like the singer Jill Scott feels her own music. In this situation, it was all about love, or was it just a bad case of being alone and desperate. Mr. Larry only showed his love by using his fist to punch on her mother's assets. This bastard-lawyer was truly out of control.

Seeing all of this at an early age, made Rachel feel uneasy about her future life expectancy. Love was supposed to be a splendid thing. Love is not supposed to hurt. Right? Another year had gone by, and winter of 1989 was approaching fast. Rachel's mother had made up her mind to let this man go, and walk away from her dead end six-year relationship.

Rachel remembered when her mother did try to leave Larry. (Flash back). She picks up the phone and calls Larry. She wanted him to meet her at her apartment as soon as he gets off work. She was nervous and shaking at the same time. Her adrenaline starts to race and her skin pale and frail. She knew that this was something that had to be done, and quick. She had to fix her situation and move on with life, or should she just remain Larry's human punching bag.

"Hey, hey, hello baby. Listen, I really need to talk to you"

"About what? Is everything okay? Larry tries to sound concerned. While she was on the phone, she could hear background conversation and paper shuffling.

"Yes? No?" She pauses and places her hands on her forehead. "We need to talk about us". Then Larry rudely cuts in, as if she was taking too much of his time because he had to get back to work.

"About us? What's the problem now? Are you planning to leave again?

"I just think we have gotten too deep too soon. You know how your wife is. She is always calling the apartment now, and she even tried to follow us after dinner from the restaurant. I know she knows the truth about us. How long are you going to pretend that she expects you are going out on business dinners?

"After six years of being with you woman, I think she would have found out by now. Damn! What are you concerned for? You did not seem to care before. And besides, it did not stop you from jumping into my bed".

"Larry, you took me to a hotel".

"It doesn't matter what bed I had you in. You still came running to me when I whistled". She takes a minute and a short breath to absorb what Larry had just said to her. She is surprised at how his whole attitude was starting to change dramatically. It was hurtful and much uncalled for.

"When you whistled?" She slowly collects her thoughts and quietly gasps for another breath. She takes the phone away from her ear. Then she places the phone back up to her ear. "Okay, okay, I'm done with your crap. I'm tired. I don't want to see you anymore. Do you hear me! I need a man who is going to love and respect me, you sorry piece of shit".

Rachel's mother is furious and this time ready to get out. Larry bangs his fist on his desk and crunches even closer to his desk phone. His tone becomes rough. He was pissed by what she had said.

"Respect you! Respect you! You think you are so high and mighty just cause your black ass is a nurse by day! Well check this out; you are my personal whore by night. So, I will tell you when you can leave. And right now, I'm not going to entertain this juvenile conversation".

"How can you do this to me? She starts to cry and her heart begins to beat louder like a drummer playing a drum.

"Do what! I'm only doing what you allowed me to do. Nothing more, always less. Just in case I need to refresh your memory, if you try to leave me, I'll break you. And you can take that however you want". Her crying grew louder over the phone lines. She felt like it was nothing that she could do.

"I have a daughter. I don't want her to think that this is how life is supposed to be I don't..." Larry had quickly intercepted and she was automatically trained to keep quiet, when he speaks.

"Hey! You made that judgment call when you brought me and my screwed up situation into both of your sick, wasted, disgusting lives. So too bad for you. Boo-who, I'll pray for your daughter".

Larry feels no remorse at all for her. She is his trophy for as long as he wants her to be. He was not letting her go under no circumstances.

"That's not fair". She continues to cry and plead for her freedom. Larry did not play fair and this was something that she did not pick up on until now. Yet then again, if your desperate think you ***need*** a man bad enough, you will put up with anything.

"Oh, it's fair. Now, get yourself a drink, and when I get there, I'm going to teach you how to be nice to your man. You see, I'm going to have to show you, better than I can tell you".

Later that night, Larry stopped by the apartment. He was high as a kite. He is so high; he begins to see various colors dancing around in his head, while he walks down the hall to get to the apartment door. He wobbles up to the door and bangs on it. The banging was so loud it caused other neighbors to look out of their own doors. Her mother was sitting on her sofa. She did not hear him at first because she was watching television, while Rachel was in the back room knocked out sleep. He bangs even louder than before. She is startled by the banging on the door and quickly jumps to her feet.

She tip-toes quietly toward the door and leans into it, to see out of the peep-hole. She sees Larry's large red blood shot eyes rolling around. He looks like he has been on a bad roller coaster ride that was invented by a mad doctor waiting for his next fix. His tie is crooked and his shoe strings are half way tied. He was sweating heavily and lips were dry. She wanders what type of ice-cream (coke) he had tasted this time. The drugs he used to take never made him look this bad. She is almost afraid to open the door. He continues to bang on the door again.

"Let me in!" She knows that she has to do something, because if she didn't let him in, Rachel will wake up, or the cops would be charging up the stairs as fast as you can say 1-2-3 red light.

"Okay, okay, just wait a minute. I have to grab my house coat" She slowly approaches the door. She looks out of the peep-hole again. Larry is leaning up against the door. She could hear his heavy breathing and long-winded sighs. One by one she opened each of the locks very, very carefully. She begins to sweat on her forehead. She is nervous and her hand starts to shake. Before she pulls back the last lock, she takes her right hand and wipes the dripping sweat from her temples. Finally, she opens the door to let Larry in.

He almost falls into the apartment, because he was leaning on the door. The door swings open and knocks against the door of the apartment.

"What took you so long to answer the door?"

"Well, I was asleep. I'm very tired from work and I fell asleep on the couch."

"Oh…you fell asleep? Or maybe someone was holding you down, and you couldn't get up."

She begins to get an attitude and turns away from the door, while Larry is still standing in the doorway. "What kind of comment is that supposed to be? You're drunk, high, or something. You're crazy to say such a thing." He starts to laugh at her, holding his stomach with a free hand, while the other hand was balled tightly. He walks into the living room and places his left foot on the coffee table and throws his Burberry suit jacket on the floor. He talks with a drunken slur and starts to foam a little at the corners of his mouth.

"What do you have to talk to big daddy about?"

She quickly speaks up without even letting Larry finish his words. "I want out. I don't want this type of life with you anymore. Look Larry, I know you do not want to be with me anymore." Larry's blood shot eyes widen as he looks at her. He starts to shake his head in disgust, as if he is blown away by what she says to him. He drunkenly walks up to her and aggressively grabs both of her arms tight. He pulls her close to his sweaty face. His nostrils wide and runny like a heated bull on a hot summer night.

"What! I love you girl. I gave you almost anything you've wanted!" She pulls away from him and takes a few steps back towards the kitchen counter. There was a box of steak- knives set up on the counter.

Lord, she prayed that she did not have to use one. So just for her safety, she lays one hand on the counter next to the knives.

"Almost? Almost did not keep the bills paid around here. Almost did not keep my lonely heart from aching, when you're not around, and almost damn sure did not put a ring on my finger, you sorry bastard." Larry suddenly approaches her and stands in her face. His anger is starting to boil. His temple starts to jump up and down. He now sees nothing but the illusions of hate in his head. "She don't want you no more. She's tired of your games, you're finished. You ain't the man no more." The illusions start to immaturely sing to him. The drugs are starting to take completely over his mind. "It's over now, you did her wrong, it's over now, get your drunk ass out of her home, it's over now, you're burned out and it's time to go to your own home, you sorry bastard". Larry starts to furiously yell at her.

"Is this what this is all about? A ring! I'm married! Married!"

"Yeah. You're right." She walks over to the door and opens it. "Good bye".

"Good bye? Good bye? He shockingly looks at her. "You're telling me good bye? See ya'?"

"Yes. I'm telling you good bye". She opens the door wider as he prepares to walk out. He slowly reaches into his pocket, pulls out a gun and points it directly in her face. She looks at him with disgust.

"Go ahead, pull the trigger. Maybe I'm better off dead, since you can't love me the way I want to be loved. I'd rather go straight to hell". She stands there with a cold look, waiting and wandering what he's going to do next.

"Wow and leave your daughter behind?" BANG! BANG! BANG! He pulls the trigger, shooting her right between the eyes and she falls to the floor. He looks at her on the floor now in a pool of blood. He hears a squeaking noise coming from one of the bedrooms. It is her daughter watching out from the crack in the door. She is shaking and crying out loud. He turns and coldly walks out of the apartment. Rachel's door now swings completely open and she walks slowly into the living room. She sees her mother lying on the floor covered with blood.

"Mommy" she sobs. "Mommy, please get up! Please mommy" sob, sob comes from her shaking voice. She leans over her mother, places her head on her mother's chest to see if she is still breathing. "MOMMY!!!!" She screams out loud.

The neighbors run in the apartment and sees Rachel slumped over her mother, all covered in blood. "OH GOD!!! Call 911! Somebody please, help us!!!"

CHAPTER 2

Rachel never forgot about that horrible night. The tragic end of how her mother died is too much for her to bear. Each night she would wake up in a cold sweat, shaking and holding herself tight. After her mother was laid to rest, she was placed in her grandma's care in Trenton, New Jersey. Rachel felt lonely at times, but her grandmother always reminded her time and time again that, "When your friends are not around, God is here for you". Rachel will always remember her grandmother's soothing and encouraging words.

Today, Rachel is a vibrant and ambitious young woman, whose height is 5'6. She weighs only 165 pounds and has a pear shape frame. Her lips are a round full shape and her lovely china-shape brown colored eyes stand out. Sometimes she wears gray contacts to make her eyes look like a sexy kitty cat on the prowl. Every time she has those gray contacts in her eyes, the young heads on the campus would go wild. The fellas would whistle, try to talk slick and make comments like "Oh girl, you make me wanna' leave the girl I'm with and start a new relationship with you".

Some of the guys on campus were immature little boys who were basically not getting much of anything, except for middle-fingers that seems to go up in the air when they are in someone's presence, especially those who were really not interested.

Rachel works out three times a week and her dark toned arms, buttocks and legs were firm. The workouts helped ease her mind and body. Now she is graduating from Spellman College and excited that she made it through. Before attending college, she encountered jealousy from other envious girls at her old high school that did not have a clue about what their future plans were going to be. To be frank, they didn't care.

Rachel was mostly quiet and kept to herself. She was not the best dresser, and her hair was not of the **INDIAN** family. She has a beautiful spirit. Her style, attitude and grace, was a heart of gold. Everywhere

Rachel went; other people would just take to her. They would see a light in her that would blossom from the top of the highest mountain. Rachel was just a kind and very considered person, who enjoyed helping people. She never looked at her kindness as a way of getting something in return, unlike some people.

There were only a few girlfriends that Rachel considered to be real friends from high-school. She faithfully rolled with her crew, Eastern, Angela, and Taneya. All four of them were like sisters. They always had each other's back, and never messed with another's man. Eastern was almost a splitting image of Rachel. The two of them would tell people that their twins and they do not play, if you were to mess with one of them. Angela was like a close cousin and sister-in-spirit. She knew Rachel very well. Now, these two went to bat for each other and helped each other through some rough times, while in and out of high school. To this day, Rachel and Angela, still keep in touch.

Now, as for Taneya, she was a different type of species. Taneya was the top-of-the line video vixen, yet in her own little way she had a heart. Taneya used to always take Rachel to private parties, out-of-town malls, and meet the banging money-making dudes on the bricks. Taneya was a sharp dresser and an enormous creator of fashion. She also had her own set of friends, but they were too "***Tha Bomb***", to hang out with Rachel. The first time that Rachel decided to go out with Taneya and her friends, they talked about Rachel's clothes and her hair. They felt that she was not dressed diva enough to go to the "Diva Fashion Show". Rachel wore a loose, one-piece, strapless black dress that hung to her knees and some casual brown tie-up sandals, with a flat heel. This style was appealing to Rachel. Why? Because she was comfortable in her own skin and did not worry about what people had to say.

It was 90 degrees that evening and it was the perfect time to be comfortable, and not sweaty. Rachel felt that this dress was to her liking and she did not want to change. Of course, in Taneya's mind, she did not approve of the way Rachel was dressed, yet, she did not mention it to Rachel, because she felt that Rachel's feelings would be hurt. Taneya knew that the dress was not an "Oscar" winning look, but she almost felt glad that Rachel wore that dress, because Rachel did not out shine her.

Taneya was definitely the type that had to always be the show- stopper. She claimed to have true friendship love for Rachel, but deep down inside, she envied Rachel for being herself. As time went on, Taneya became more and more jealous of Rachel on the down low. She always wondered how Rachel can do that with such small change. "Why is everyone so big on her? She is nothing, have nothing, and probably will never be nothing".

Rachel was at the top of her senior class, and was on the honor roll 2 years straight. During Rachel's final year of high school, she went to a private school because the immature girls at her old high school, was too much like video vixens, model chicks, or get-rich-quick chicks. Rachel's mother did not want this to influence her. Plus, their grades were not on point, and Rachel had to make a decision, stay behind or move ahead.

Everybody had to be popular, in order to get with somebody, who already had five other significant others. People are not lying when they say pop goes the cherry. Cherries were popping all over the hallways, bathrooms, classrooms, staff of the building and so forth.

Times have changed and only 20% of high school graduates continued their education and went to college. As for the 80% percent of high school kids, they got local jobs, or just chose to live life as they saw fit (U Do the Math???). (Back to the PRESENT).

It's graduation day, and Rachel is waking up from her last night's sleep in her dorm room. She turns to look at the clock and sees that the time is 9:00 am. Graduation starts approximately at 10:15. This is truly going to be an exciting day for Rachel and the rest of her college buddies.

No matter what comes or goes, it will be okay. If it were to rain this very day it would still be a beautiful and blessed day. Everyone has worked hard, and is ready to walk down that isle and receive their long-awaited diplomas.

The stadium is full of family and friends sitting in the stands, right under the large tents that blocks the hot and hazy sun. Babies were crying, swinging their arms and kicking, trying to get down out of their parent's arms, so they could run wild on the beautiful green grass. The band was playing "Ain't No Stopping Us Now" and the color guards were twirling the flags around shouting, "It's gonna be alright, just do it, do it You can do it!!!". On the other side of the stands the freshman, sophomores and some juniors came out to show their support and amazement of what to look forward to when it's their time to get their diplomas.

Rachel stares out into the crowd and sees her sixty-nine, year-old grandmother. She's every bit of 5 feet, 5 inches tall and very petite. Her beautiful caramel complexion shines off of her high cheek bones. Her bluish-gray eyes were radiant and her posture was fierce. Her grandmother smiles as she sits in her seat, holding her chest with one hand and a bushel of flowers in the other. There was an empty seat next to her grandmother, with a graduation program placed neatly beside her. No one sat there. Rachel slowly gazes up at the clear blue sky; her mind begins to wander about her own mother sitting there all smiles, excited to see her baby take her next step onto her GWS "Grown Woman Status".

"My mother could have been sitting right there, or maybe my father. But it's okay, my grandmother's there. I love you mommy, with all my heart and soul. So much I wished for you to see me grow and be this great role model. Right? I pray every-day that nothing or no one will try to make me do something that will hurt me, or hurt myself. I don't knock you for being you. Yes, you did your best and now it's time for me to take care of the rest."

She slowly positions her head straight, wipes her tears and adjust her graduation cap. "Thank you Jesus for allowing my grandmother to be here on this very day to see me graduate".

Her grandmother took care of her until she was able to take care of herself. She kept her clean, fed and shaped her into a beautiful young lady. She taught Rachel how to speak, walk and act the way a real young lady should conduct herself. Most important, she wanted her grand-daughter to love herself, love God and try to stay in the word of God. She insisted that Rachel read her bible every night, while she was away in college. Of course, everyone knows that when you go away somewhere, away from home, a large amount of peer-pressure can come into play.

Rachel never ignored what her grandmother asked of her, she just prayed to God and asked HIM to guide her in the right direction. After a while the audience could hear the band plays the music selection for the ceremony to introduce the graduates. they stand to their feet to receive their diplomas. This day is perfect to see so many different nationalities joining together to graduate from college. When everyone's name is being called the proud graduates steps up to the podium, receive their diplomas and take pictures. Parents scream out loud to their sons and daughters and honk their loud horns to show their support.

Once all of the graduates received their piece of paper, the guest speaker gave them the signal to turn their tonsils to the other side of their caps. When the final word is spoken, the graduates take off their caps; throw it up in the air and yells "Yessss! I'm finally out of here!!!" Rachel looks around at everyone hugging and kissing, sending off their condolences and farewells.

"Yes. The real world awaits us. Ready "R"? Let's go get em'" says her brainiac college buddy and best friend, Nia Closely-Carter. Nia's degree was for Elementary education and Child psychology. Nia is an extremely beautiful African-American young lady, mixed with Italian, Hispanic and a touch of Jamaican. She is 6 feet tall and weighs approximately 175 pounds. She's somewhat slim, shapely but very sophisticated. No matter how beautiful she is, Nia would always get her feelings hurt by past boy-friends, envious friends, and even next of kin-friends. Some of the fellas on campus would say how beautiful she is, and how she almost looks like Halle Berry, sexy, but crazy as HELL!!!

All through college Rachel and Nia stuck together and had each other's back. They helped each other with school work, personal problems and weathered the storm together when times get rough. Even though Nia is two years older than Rachel, she respected her for sharing her opinions and treated her like a sister she always wanted. Of course, some students were jealous of their friendship because they were so close and smart too. Sometimes folks didn't want to see others happy. Nia is also working on building a closer relationship with God. She was taught by her own parents to still treat people well, even if they try to give you all types of hell. Still treat your brothers and sisters with nothing but love and respect.

Rachel and Nia stayed in the same room, ate the same food and their style of dress was the same. Yet they never dated the same guy. That was not the cool thing to do. U C, everyone ain't gangsta boos. They were like sisters, beautiful, intelligent, young ladies who want a career, family and MO Money. It's the American dream. Right? After the ceremony, the two of them embrace each other with a long hug and say their good-byes.

"Nia, I'm going to miss you girl"

"Rachel, just because we live a few thousand miles apart, does not mean we can't visit each other. You know you're always welcome in my home Rachel. The offer still stands. Jump on a plane, train, bus. Just get there. My family and I got you. Know that". Rachel looks at Nia as if she wanted to tell her something real about her part of time. (U Do the Math!!!).

"You're right Nia". Rachel pauses and Nia cuts in before she could finish.

"Hey girl, as long as we have God on our side, our friendship, now sisterhood will never fade. Well, unless death come into play" says Nia playfully as she shrugs her shoulders against Rachel's. "But listen, you will always be my sista girl, no matter what, okay?". Nia leans in closer and hugs Rachel. This time it's tighter than the first.

"You know something Nia, God will definitely show you who your real friends are and those scaly wag boyfriends will be out of your flesh and a new man will be coming through". Nia starts to laugh.

"Well, he better hurry up because my flesh is about to go somewhere God might not want to bring me out of". They both laugh and say their final good-byes. Rachel did not want to part from her close friend and new found sister, but other plans were
now in motion at this time. Rachel has to go back home with her grandmother, work on finding a decent job, but until then she has to mooch off of her grandmother for a while. Sad, but happy hugs and good-byes is exchanged and the girls go their separate ways.

"We're gonna keep in touch, right Rachel? I have your address and number" Nia says as she walks toward her parents waiting patiently the chauffeur to open the door of the black 2011 Range Rover.

"Yeah, I have your information too Nia. Hey you know what? I really had a great time with you and I'm glad we became good friends" Nia smiles, gets into the Range and rolls the window down to respond back.

"Thanks Girl! So, keep in touch, okay".

Rachel turns towards her grandmother, walks up to her, takes her hand and goes back towards the dorm to gather up the rest of her things. Once the room is all cleared out, she returns her key to the dorm attendant. Grandma Agnes grabs two small leather bags, heads out of the dorm, and looks for the black Lincoln continental that's supposed to be park out front ready and waiting. She got a great deal with the car and the driver. *They're related.* Lol smiley faces (U Do the Math!!!). The ghetto, thugged out Lincoln pulls in front of the dorm. It had shiny 20-inch star rims, dark tinted windows with a loud sound system playing "*Ain't no woman like the one*

I got". The inside of the car's interior is cream and dark purple, with stylish white wall tires. The driver is good ole' Uncle Skeet. A real OG. Omega Psi Phi, "Q-Dog". Graduated back in 1965 and still hasn't used his degree since. He majored in Engineering and Economics. He's smart, makes his money on the low and no taxes. This saved him a lot of money. He doesn't use a bank account. He uses his trusty old mattress.

He sees Grandma Agnes and Rachel approaching the car. He quickly jumps out of the car and excitedly greets Rachel. He is a short guy, weighs about 189 pounds and is 5 feet tall and 2 inches high. He used to be in shape, but now he's got more back than J-Lo. Yet his friends say he's very light on his feet, when he dances. He has a huge smile as he reaches out to shake Rachel's hand and give her a kiss on the cheek.

"Well, well, well. My niece is beau-ti-ful, mmm, mmm, mmm". He starts to sing and do a two-step from side to side. (freaking clown). "Beau-ti-ful, I just want you to know you're my favorite girlllll". He takes a quick pause and looks at Rachel, trying to get her attention.

"Girlllll! Damn! You look fine. Come here and let me kiss you one more time". Grandma Agnes intervenes this time and steps in front of Uncle Skeet.

"Now just hold up, Lil' Skeeter-Peeter, coke sniffer and pickle eater. You better back up and take these bags or else you'll be kissing my MRS. 45, and trust, for THE LAST TIME!!! Do you understand the words that are seeping through my dentures, you broke bastard!"

Uncle Skeet looks at Grandma Agnes, bends down to pick up the rest of the luggage and snoots his noise up like a prissy woman on Hollywood Blvd. Rachel tosses the left-over groceries in the trash and the last piece of luggage into the trunk of the limo. Then all three of them get into the limo and head for the airport. Uncle Skeet is so excited to finally meet Rachel. She was one of the kin folks, that never told Uncle Skeet where to stick the bull crap that usually comes out of his mouth.

Uncle Skeet always had a way of making people say harsh things to him, and he could never understand why. Well, as for her grandmother, she is definitely one of those folks who would give you a piece of her mind immediately. A long time ago, Uncle Skeet gave away Grandma Agnes beautiful vase, along with her beautiful yellow flowers to some woman that he was trying to get with. Grandma Agnes felt that he could have at least used one of his own pickle jars. He could have used one of his old pickle jars for beer. So why not for flowers?

Uncle Skeet gave away an expensive multi-colored Chinese vase. He promised that he was going to return the vase just as soon as the flowers died and replace it with fresh flowers. He said the wrong thing to Grandma Agnes. Her face frowned up like a five-day old prune, waiting to explode.

"Freshhhhhhh". It rolled off his tongue like a mint cooling bad breath. Uncle Skeet claimed that the flowers he took were almost half dead. So, he thought that he was doing her a favor and get rid of them for her. After he gave his so-called girlfriend the flowers, she turned around and gave them to her other man as a belated birthday present. Uncle Skeet's girl-friend used him like a crack-head trying to sell a vacuum cleaner at full price.

This woman caused Uncle Skeet stress, go into to hibernation and live like a grizzly bear without his honey. No one saw Uncle Skeet for weeks. He had given this woman the best two days of his life. He used to take her to dinner at Arby's and supply her with California coolers. He was chilling in his one-bedroom apartment. This was what Uncle Skeet considered top notch romancing for his ladies (Freaking Nut-bucket).

Now Uncle Skeet's single, insecure and very unhappy. Grandma Agnes still fumes at the thought of what he had done to her. Rachel leans in close toward her grandmother's face and slightly touches her shoulder.

"Grandma, is it that serious? Come on there is going to come a time when you are going to have to let go of the past". Her grandmother shakes her head in disgust.

"Let Go! Why do I have to be the one to bend! This short rump of dried up burned B-B-Q ribs took a very expensive item from me". Uncle Skeet looks at Grandma Agnes and begins to chuckle under his breath.

"Come on Agnes! Precious? Expensive? Okay, I can see precious, but expensive. You only bought it for $2 at the "Lord Have Mercy Spot" (Red, White and the blue). The clerk should have charged you more after you pulled up one of your polyester pants legs and showed him your old run-down knee caps". Rachel quickly cut into the conversation.

"Why are you still so angry? Uncle Skeet appears to be a sweetheart". Rachel tries to bring a cheerful atmosphere to a hot and steamy unresolved situation. Her grandmother turns to her and begins to state her case.

"He's more like a sour heart with "Super-Sucker" written across his receding hairline. He shouldn't let people use him like a cheap trick at freak-nik. The dumb bastard that he is". Rachel shakes her head and giggles a little to herself.

"A…grandma, please tell me you did not take that line Lil Kim used in her rhyme?" Grandma Agnes looks at her granddaughter with a confused look. What was Rachel talking about?

"Lil Kim? Who is Lil Kim? I heard that saying from Big Jim who owns the corner bar on Willow Street, along with Tiny Slim, the barber from Spring Street Barber Shop. By the way, Tiny Slim is kin folk too". Grandma pauses for a minute and scratch her chin." Now wait a minute, is this Lil Kim the same little nasty girl that had one of her breasts flapping out of her skin tight jumper on national TV?" Grandma Agnes chuckles to herself and says "I love that Lil Kim".

Uncle Skeet continues to look at Grandma Agnes in his rear-view mirror, frowning, twisting and clutching his teeth. He turns his head several times from left to right, up and down, waiting for the right time to cut in.

"Here we go again. If you can't say nothing nice, ya' beatle-juice misfit, then don't say nothing at all". The two of them begin to bicker back and forth. Without thinking, Uncle Skeet takes his focus off the road, turns around towards Grandma Agnes and waves his pointer finger in her face. She quickly reaches out her hand trying to grab his finger, but he pulls back his hand before she could get a hold of it.

The car begins to swerve out of control. Uncle Skeet quickly turns around, grabs the wheel and gains control of the car. Rachel intercepts the situation again. She yells at both of them to stop.

"Oh God! What is wrong with you two!!! Uncle Skeet keep your eyes on the road!!!". He pulls the car to the side of the gravel road. The car takes a few seconds to stop, does a 360 finally coming to a complete stop.

Everyone was quiet and looking around to see if a police car was on its way to pull up behind them, makes them get out of the car and do an alcohol test. Once again Uncle Skeet looks at Grandma Agnes and begins to fume like a sweaty heated bull ready to take on its competition. The stem pops off of his bald head like a hot smokey B-B-Q rib flaming on Aunt Ellen's grill.

He clinches his fist tight and begins to shake it at Grandma Agnes. Aunt Ellen is Grandma Agnes's sister from Wishy-Washy Georgia. (Talk about that story another time).

"Woo, look at that. Your head is so hot; I can cook a cheese egg on that joker. Hell, maybe two". Grandma laughs out loud, slapping Rachel on her tired shoulders. As she leans in closer towards Uncle Skeet, she tries to touch his head!

"Oh man, do you think I can get a pickle or a side dish of bacon with those eggs, ya' dumb bastard! How bout' it Rachel? As hot as his head is, you could probably get a steak well done, medium rare. How bout' Cajun style? Or do you college kids prefer turkey burgers?"

Uncle Skeet's eyes begin to turn red like fire. Sweat trickles down the left side of his face and his lips starts to shake uncontrollably. They can hear his back teeth grind away like a train chuckling down the track. His temples pounds in and out of the side of his head like a drum. His temperature shoots up so high nearly causing a blood vessel to burst in his brain (Clown for real). Uncle Skeet continues to stare at Grandma Agnes because he's definitely at his last grips with her annoying, selfish, inconsiderate self.

He looks at Rachel as she sits there quiet looking at the two of them, acting like the children of the corn and their cousins belonged to the bride of chucky. Uncle Skeet rolls his eyes at Rachel's grandmother, looks up at the roof of his car as if he is searching for Jesus to come down and slap her grandmother with a scripture.

"God. Now ya' know I'm trying my best to ignore Satan's demon seed. Her insane ways are not yours and she's driving me batty, I want to drink an entire bottle of Tequila and then eat the worm".

Rachel takes in a deep breath, puckers her lips, and slowly blows out air. Her grandmother focuses her eyes on Rachel, pats her on the leg and then softly push back the loose strands hanging on her grand-daughter's forehead.

"Rachel baby, I'm sorry. This is supposed to be a celebration, your graduation day. And that tub-of-lard uncle of yours is screwing it all up". Rachel lashes out.

"Can we just get to the airport? This arguing doesn't make any sense. We're supposed to be family, not folks who just fell off a banana boat with monkeys. Guess what? I think the monkeys won (Intelligence for their butts).

"Please. Family? Family died when he stole my vase with those beautiful flowers in it". And the saga continues…

"That was years ago Agnes. I thought you were going to let that go".

"Let it go! Let it go! When you figure out why your pathetic love life went sour, then I'll let it go". Uncle Skeet begins to wave his finger at her.

"You know what Agnes? You need Jesus and the parting of the red sea on your" Rachel cuts in.

"Uncle Skeet!!!"

"I was gonna say; before I console with her old stinking butt". Grandma Agnes laughs out loud.

"And you need Listerine for your thirty-year old gingivitis, Mr. Jelly-bowl man".

The two of them starts to bicker again and time is running out. The plane will be taking off soon. Rachel throws her hands in the air.

"Will the both of you stop! Grandma we have a plane to catch, and Uncle Feet, Cheat, or whatever your name is, just please drive. Damn!!!". Her grandmother looks at her with rage in her eyes and her fists balled up.

"I just know you didn't use God's name in vain. After all I've done to raise you right". Her grandmother pauses. This gives Rachel room to quickly intercept the conversation.

"Grandma please, you only raised me until I was old enough to walk. After that you threw my mother out of the house because she dropped out of school just days before her graduation and then we moved away to New York". Her grandmother sadly put her head down because she thought that Rachel did not remember that part of her life. "My mother told me how you used to make her stay in the house and work her like a dog, so that she wouldn't grow up to be like those fast girls in the street. I hated you for that. But then I had to realize that you are the parent, and I assumed you knew what was best. My mother was a beautiful person, a nurse and scholar. She just got off on the wrong side of the tracks. But guess what? I still love her. And said she'd always love you no matter what".

Her grandmother sat in silence. Uncle Skeet starts the car, puts it in drive and heads off to the airport. The clouds begin to get dark as the breeze begins to slightly pick up, causing a few leaves to swirl around in one spot. Particles of ripped newspapers, dry leaves and dust flies in the air.

Loud sounds of thunder begin to bang in the sky like a street musician banging on his bongo and blowing his whistle. A storm is approaching fast.

Suddenly the clouds cover the gray sky and rain starts to pour down, hitting the window shield. The rain makes it almost impossible for Uncle Skeet to drive the normal speed limit.

As they finally get closer to the airport, other drivers begin to slam on their brakes and slowly coast down the airport's mini highway.

It seemed like the limo ride took forever to get to the airport and the traffic was starting to get a bit suspect. Not too busy, but just enough cars that's moving slow, to make the limo ride longer. As they arrived, the airport traffic lights were taking longer to change and now car horns are blowing all over the place. People were getting ticked off and saying heated words that could even make the devil think twice about coming up for cool air. Uncle Skeet turns on the radio to block out some of the disturbance. Cars were slowly approaching both sides of the limo. You could see children in one car jumping up and down, losing their minds and in another car an elderly woman clutching the steering wheel tight. LOL! She was going two miles per hour.

Uncle skeet sees an open lane, and proceeds to move over to try and get pass the other cars. Actually, it's a closed lane where there's construction work taking place at the airport. Uncle Skeet always keeps his old dusty construction hat on stand-by, just in case an emergency comes up. While driving along the side of the mini highway, he hits several large pot holes, nearly missing a hidden ditch that could take the whole front end of his car apart.

The construction worker looks up and notices Uncle Skeet swiftly moving down the restricted path. One of the workers steps in the road holds up a red stop sign and cautions for Uncle Skeet to stop. He hand-signals for him to pull over. Uncle Skeet stops the car and rolls down his window.

"Excuse me sir, but this road is for non-moving traffic. Uh, can't you see it's a mess on this side of the road?" Uncle Skeet looks at the man with a shaky but stern look. His fingers start to tap on the steering wheel like he's playing the keys on a baby grand piano. (Playskool…that is).

"Hello, how are you sir? Messy day we're having"

"Uh sir, you're in an authorized area. You shouldn't be on this side of the road. Please move your car immediately". Uncle Skeet stays put and acts like he's the man.

"No. I'm not gonna' move. I see construction workers, the sign says construction workers ahead and I'm a construction worker tryna' get ahead of this traffic, so I can get to work on some uh, uh, you know construction work, partna'"".

The construction worker scratches his hairy chin and leans into the car window, and looks Uncle Skeet right in his eyes.

"And you're a construction worker? From where? Fruits Ville, ya' country bamma".

"That's right. I don't live in Fruits Ville. They got a name where I'm from Playboy"

Kyra and her grandmother look on as Uncle Skeet tries to get over on the man.

"I was sent out here to make sure that you gentlemen are doing what you're supposed to be doing". He pulls out an old expired work ID, quickly flashes it in the man's face and then places it back into his wallet. "Now, if I may ask you a question? Why are you still standing here? Don't you have some holes to fill, work to do, work to doooooooo?". Uncle Skeet tries to sound like the actor Martin Lawrence, but this was not the day, or so *he* thought.

The security police proceed slowly behind the Uncle Skeet's limo. He sees the police car in his rear-view mirror. He pulls out a twenty-dollar bill from his jacket and now tries to bribe the worker to let him pass.

"Look son, my niece just graduated from college and we're trying to catch a flight back home. It's been a while since I've seen her and she needs to catch up on old times with the family. You understand, right? You know, it's all about family"

Uncle Skeet really tries to spread it on thick. "So, you think I could get pass?" He tries to slide the twenty dollars to the man without the police seeing him.

"It's been a long afternoon and the Misses back there, well, let's just say her bowls are ready to explode". The construction worker glances up at the police, then he looks at Uncle Skeet.

"Give me a hundred ya' cheap bastard and I'll let you go"

"Oh, come on! You make more than me. I'm on social security, and they don't pay much anymore". The man slowly leans up and motions for the police officer to get out of his patrol car.

"Oh well, Excuse me officer". The worker says as he continues to gesture for the officer to close in on Uncle Skeet.

"Okay, okay. Here take it! Didn't you guys just get a raise, better pension and a health plan?". The worker hand signals the police to let them know that everything is okay, takes the money out of Uncle Skeet's hand and chuckles.

"Hell, yeah we got all that. But this here *hunnett* dollar bill is going to come in handy. I got a date with Brandy the Brazen Blueberry. Now get on out of here ya' fat cheap bastard". The man laughs as Uncle Skeet pulls off.

"Thanks. You're too kind". They finally pull off and head to the arrival section of the airport. Uncle Skeet pull up in front of the sliding glass doors, turns the ignition off and jumps out of the car, walks around to the back of the car and opens the trunk. He pulls out their luggage and takes it to the counter to check it in. Now they have to rush to get situated and get onto the plane before it takes off.

CHAPTER 3

Time is up and the plane is ready for take-off. As Uncle Skeet pulls up to the airports parking meter, he notices a long line of cars standing still. The other vehicle's motors are running, hazard lights are blinking off and on and horns are constantly honking. HONK! HONK-HONK!!!!!!!!

The drivers give each other the middle finger and gestures signs in an aggressive manner. "Get out of the way!!! Keep it moving!!! I'm late for work Idiot!!! Wow. Everyone is in a rush to make their flight. People are walking fast in all directions of the airport and security is posted at the entrance and exit doors. Everyone has to have their luggage scanned, searched and then wait for an approval to pass through the security both.

Announcements for flight departures are announced every ten to fifteen minutes. So far all of the flights appear to be running on time. People of different nationalities are

resting in the lounge areas and dinning areas. The restrooms and bar are crowed with folks preparing themselves to depart. Small children are running around the waiting
area, playing tag and hide and seek while their parents and other patrons sit back and read magazines or the daily newspaper.

At the other end of the airport a bunch of rowdy high school jocks and cheerleaders with their fancy varsity jackets on parades around the tasty peanut stand. They proudly sing their victory song (Over, and over and over and over). When they finish singing and cheering the on-lookers clap, whistle and then clap some more.

Rachel reaches in her tiny over stuffed purse, pulls out her airline tickets and hands it over to Grandma Agnes. She fumbles a little trying not to drop anything out of her M G designer wallet, she purchased from Macy's last spring.

"This wallet is so cute, yet so expensive. Well, if you like it then splurge on it". Rachel picks up both the bags and carries it for her grandmother.

"Oh baby, I can carry that I'm not cripple". Her grandmother says with a smile.

"Well, it's okay. The bags look like its hurting your back. It's really not a problem". Rachel proceeds to take the bags from her grandma.

"Well help me by giving me back ma' back. I see a cutie standing over there by the vending machine checking out all my fineness. You know a man just loves to see a woman with strength". Grandma Agnes takes her bag back and props it over her shoulder and smiles. She tries to silently grunt from the pain in her shoulder. She looks at Rachel and gives her a sneaky smile, knowing she is in pain.

"Uh, are you okay grandma? You look like that shoulder is giving you a problem". Rachel laughs. Her grandmother begins to look sluggish and her breathing begins to get heavy. She finally takes the bag off of her shoulder and hands it over to Rachel.

"Here, he's gone anyway. You can only be strong for so long. Then you got to ask God to give you more strength to make it through the rest of the hour, maybe minute if ya' nasty". Her grandmother chuckles at herself. Rachel smiles at her grandmother. (God bless her grandmother's little ole' heart).

"It's okay grandma. We all get tired sometimes and need a little nudge to carry us through". They finally board the plane and hand the airline stewardess their boarding tickets. Late travelers quickly board the plane and take their seats. Chit chat is heard throughout the plane.

One of the women on the plane notices Rachel's funky MG wallet as she walks towards her direction. Rachel takes a seat right across from the woman. The woman takes a sip of her cognac and begins to have a conversation with her husband.

"That is a lovely dress that young lady has on. Isn't it dear?". Her husband is focusing on the game on his cell phone. "Dear did you hear me? Never mind. Hey! A football!". Her husband looks up and sees that there's no football in sight. "Psycho wife", he says to himself. The woman leans towards Rachel and pats her on the wrist.

"Hey sweetie, that's a pretty dress. Where you headed? To Jamaica?". Rachel looks over at the woman.

"Thank you"

"Oh yeah that dress is numeral Uno baby. Did you get it from Jamaica? You didn't answer that question".

"Oh, I'm sorry, didn't mean to be rude. No. I got the dress from Fossil collection". Rachel turns her head towards the front and puts her earphones on.

"I really like the colors. It's so colorful. It has blue, white, with a touch of apricot orange to match your purse. Are you sure you didn't get that dress from Jamaica?". She taps Rachel on the wrists again.

"I'm sorry did you say something?"

"Yes. I said are you sure you didn't get it from Jamaica? Cause it looks like Jamaica to me mon'. Ha, ha!". Rachel pulls off her earphones.

"No. I told you I got it from Fossil". The woman's husband tries to help Rachel out by placing his hand over his wife's flapping mouth.

"Sandy, ya' talk too much. Leave the girl alone. She told you already where she got the damn dress, ya' pesty witch. Boy, I can't take you anywhere. Didn't you learn your lesson from the last plane ride? Before the plane landed, you had a restraining order and a lawsuit, ya' big dummy!". The woman knocks her husband's hand away from her mouth.

"Move Sam, let the pretty lady sit over here. I want to get a closer look at her dress. Move it ya' pork eater!". Rachel looks around wondering, "What does this woman want from me?". The woman's husband gets up and shakes his head. He looks over at Rachel and politely gestures for her to sit in his seat, just until he comes from the bathroom.

"Please. If you don't talk to her, she'll get rowdy. I don't like rowdy. Please take my seat". He passes Rachel some ear plugs. "Here you go. Slide these in your ears and just say yes to everything. She'll get tired after a while". Rachel takes the earplugs and slides them in her pocket. She gets up from her seat and sits with the woman.

"So, what's your destination? Chicago? Aruba? Jamaica? All the pretty girls go to Jamaica?". Rachel shakes her head and sighs.

"No. Actually, I'm going home to New Jersey"

"You know what? My best friend is sleeping with her best friend's ex-husband". Rachel raises her eyebrows and shakes her head as she listens to this out of the blue story.

"Really". Rachel says in an uninterested tone.

"Yeah, and they went to Jamaica to get their groove back on, or something like that". The woman continues to talk in a drunken slur tone. "And a trip to Jamaica can only mean two things". Rachel cuts in.

"Hey Ms. I don't think I want to hear this. You seem like a really nice lady, who just needs to get a nap. It's going to be okay. Just take a nap and in a couple of hours you'll feel great". Rachel gets up and returns to her seat next to her grandma. The woman yells out to Rachel.

"Hey! Ya' got a dollar?"

"Excuse me"

"Nothing". Her husband finally returns from the bathroom.

"My God honey, what are you doing?"

"Nothing. Sweet girl. She's sweet, right honey?". She pats her husband on his knee.

"Yeah, yeah. You need to sleep off that alcohol"

"Whatever man. You need to take me to Jamaica Mon!"

Rachel stares out of the airplane window. The clouds move slowly across the sky. The thought of leaving new friends behind makes her a bit sad. The advantage of being around positive people made a difference in her life. It was always good to be associated with ambitious hardworking people instead of folk with bad attitudes and crushed dreams.

People who think they are better than others were nothing but followers, trying to chase someone else's dream. She turns away from the window, looks at her grandmother and watches her as she tries to put her shoe back on her foot. She begins to chuckle to herself. It's so funny to see her grandmother trying to hang with the best. "This momma still got it going on. It's love. Only a grandchild can give that much to a woman like Grandma Agnes. I guess I can say she tried with my mom. I don't know"

Slight turbulence rocks the plane and a look of concern quickly races across the passengers faces. The flight attendant calmly picks up the radio mic.

"Now ladies and gentlemen, please stay calm. It's only a slight turbulence that will pass shortly. The crew is doing everything possible to get you safely to your destination. Please stay in your seats and keep your seat belts buckled until further notice. Thank you".

A man's voice burst out, talking loud and obnoxious from his seat.

"Hey lady! I'm not trying to be sarcastic but too many planes have gone down already. So, don't tell me to calm down. I'm releasing all kinds of bodily fluid in my diaper right now. Sorry". His comment to the flight attendant causes some tension amongst the other passengers.

"Hey! I bet ya' didn't check the woman with the oversized lunch bag, did you? They don't make jelly sandwiches like that anymore, or do they?". The people on the plane were starting to become disruptive and very disrespectful towards one another. The flight attendant tried to be cordial towards everyone's request, but some folk are just plain ignorant.

"Sir, please keep it down. You're scaring the other passengers". She says in a calm voice as she walks up to the man, handing him a vodka and scotch to calm his nerves. The rude man continues to spark everyone on the plane.

"And lady, with breath like yours, you're liable to put me to death. Early!". The attendant walks away from the man and tend to the other passengers to see if they need any assistance. Grandma Agnes looks at Rachel and thinks to herself how proud she is of her grandchild. "She came a long way. My baby, my baby. Rachel has definitely matured into a fine young lady. Lord I hope she's been reading her bible while she was in college".

After a while the turbulence ceased and the plane ride was smooth towards the end of the flight. The plane finally reaches its destination. Upon landing in Philly, Rachel sees that nothing has changed, except for some businesses and travel since that horrible attack back on September 11, the 911 incident. Luckily her grandmother was able to get a decent flight out of New Jersey to see Rachel's graduation. If not, she would have had to drive to the graduation with serious road rage and that would not have been pretty.

It seemed like only yesterday when her grandmother would take trips to come and see Rachel and her mother. (Even though she didn't stay too long). Back in the day it was hot, humid and hazy. Grandma Agnes decided to drive instead of taking a train or a plane. She used to love to sight see while driving to and from Brooklyn, New York.

She would always stop at her favorite vintage shop on Fulton Avenue. She dazzled herself in vintage clothing and jewelry that would just make your jaw drop. She would purchase the most enticing threads and re-style them herself. At times, she took as long as three hours to decide if she should buy the clothing because she felt that it should have been a little bit cheaper. The clothing only cost ten dollars and some change.

Mr. Bob, the shop owner, would always get cranky because Grandma Agnes tried to get him to take the price down the three and a quarter. Mr. Bob would rant and rave about how cheap the prices were and then bang on his wobbly counter. He would always say, "Agnes! Please give a small business man a break. I'm tryna' make a living. Do ya' see that ole' red and orange pick-up truck outside? I'm tryna' get a new one. But I can't cause ya' always want a break. I'm struggling and ya' tryna break me down!". Grandma Agnes always had a come back line for Mr. Bob the shop owner.

"Struggling? If ya' struggling, how come I saw ya' wife driving a new Mercedes Benz around the block bout' twenty seconds ago, tryna' see who ya' got here in this busted down, insect infected store. Man, you ain't struggling ya' swindling cheap bastard"

"Look Agnes ya' gone buy something or keep running ya' mouth?". She always kept Mr. Bob's pressure up.

"Okay" she says with a devilish grin. "Okay, give this fine leather jacket to me for, say, uh four dollars". Mr. Bob always blows his top. Always.

"What! Are you crazy! This here is true leather, pure 100% leather vintage and it's not to be sold cheap. It's worth bout maybe one thousand and fifty. Yeah, that sounds bout' right. It's all that and a bag of Red Bank tobacco. No! I ain't selling". (Oh boy. Here we go).

"Oh yeah! Well, how bout I go outside and tell ole' wifey how ya' been looking' at all this big booty baby. And my thighs, even though my knee caps sit low, ya' been skeemin', tryna' get a piece of this sugar pie. Now I ain't stupid. Cause I saw ya' looking' through those popcorn glasses, with half prescription in em', ya' cheap bastard. Ha ha! Like I said, you are a cheap bastard!". Mr. Bob always ends up giving Grandma Agnes her way, even when she doesn't deserve it.

"Okay, okay. You can have it for four dollars. Now get on out of here". Mr. Bob is a sucker for real.

To this day, Grandma Agnes would strongly laugh to herself about how she quickly gathered her bag together and hurried out of that store. But of course, her grand exit wasn't over just yet. (Go back in time. Just for a minute…maybe two).

"Oh Mr. Bob, see ya' next time. Ya' cheap bastard!!!".

"Yeah! A'ight, bye! With ya' fine booty-licious looking, Oh, Lord have mercy on me. Help me Jesus, this woman gone make me lose my mind up in here, up in here" says Mr. Bob, as he shouts out while grabbing his inner thigh. (Go figure).

Thank goodness her travels played out well. Even though Grandma Agnes is a

Christian, she wasn't perfect yet still, God knows her heart. Meanwhile after reminiscing about her road rage adventures, Rachel on the other hand smiles and reaches for her grandmother's hand as the pilot prepares to land the plane.

"Why are you smiling so hard Rachel?"

"Nothing, I'm just glad that you're here. It's amazing. You've always been there for me. Although you and my mother didn't always see eye to eye, you were there. I never really took the time to say thank you". Her grandmother leans over and kisses her on the cheek.

"You're quite welcome baby. Now, I hope you're not hinting around for me to give you some cash cause grandma's all tapped out right now". The two of them laugh.

"Now why do you think that? I thought you loved me". Rachel says in a playful manner while batting her eye lashes at her grandmother.

"Oh yeah, I love ya'. I love ya' enough to knock the fire out of you when ya' playing with me". She laughs and then says to Rachel, "Baby girl. I know your heart, God knows your heart, thoughts, feelings, desires, everything you are about to say and do. And I definitely know how broke you college kids can be on and off campus, okay".

Rachel leans closer to her grandmother's cheek, wraps her arms around her and hugs her grandmother real tight.

"You're right about college kids being broke. But I'm that special crab that got out of the barrel, that's going to get a great job with a great salary and banging benefits. I'm going to take care of you, like you've taken care of me".

Her grandmother grabs a bag of peanuts and a coke soda from the unattended cart sitting in the middle of the isle. She twists off the top, and puts the soda under her nose to feel the fizzles.

"Well for starters baby, ya' whole paycheck would be nice". The both of them laugh. "But ya' know I got the huge corn sitting on ma' big toe". Grandma Agnes taps Rachel on the shoulder to see if she's listening. "Look chile! Look" her grandmother laughs as she tries to show Rachel her toe. "Are ya' listening? This corn right here".

Rachel looks around at the other passengers watching her grandmother massage her corns on the plane. "OOOWWW this feels so good". She oozes and ahhhhs, as she continues to rub her feet. "Well, it's all good in my neighborhood Rachel. I too get pedicures, manicures, waxes, oh yeah and the Brazilian waxes are the best. Ya' ever heard of French kiss? Mmmmmmuah! It's soooo good. Holla if ya' hear me! Hey, but don't hate baby girl. Congratulate! Isn't that how the young folk express themselves?"

Rachel laughs at her grandmother, scratches her head then turns to look out of the window. She sees two beautiful birds soaring in the skies as the plane gets closer to the ground for landing. The cars, trucks, buses and people moving around the airline grounds become more and more clear.

"We're about to land. It's about time, because I'm starting to get jet-lag with some fierce on-coming bowel movements ready to bust wide open"

"What?". Her attention turns to her grandchild. "Rachel what are you talking about? You see cows moving. We're not in Kansas". Rachel laughs at her grandmother.

"Grandma, when was the last time you had your ears checked? I said bowels not cows. Hello!". Her grandmother looks at her with her glasses now sitting on the tip of her nose.

"Hello? Well ring, ring, ding, ting-a-ling. Don't get smart. I'll smack ya' so hard you'd have thought that this plane went through a wild turbulence at ground level. Just like that cheap sew in you got in ya' head. Just kidding baby. But on the real, keep ya' "*Hello*" to ya' self".

"Oh boy. Do you have to always get so dramatical? I mean so far out there, way, way out there". Says Rachel as she gestures with her arms up in the air and her finger tips swirling around in front of her face.

"No. I just know when I'm right. Chick". Rachel doesn't want to argue with her grandmother, so she basically tries to kill the conversation.

"Yeah, and that's the problem. Let's just change the subject. We are almost home and I just want to relax a bit".

Grandma Agnes cuts her eye at Rachel and sucks her false teeth. Her eyes begin to turn a fiery red. Gray strands start to stand up straight and her fists are slightly balled up. (Agnes always ready for battle).

"Yeah? Keep on talking junk and you'll be relaxing in the luggage compartment. Yeah, with ya' mouth wide open and everything else goes to south, ya' heard". The airline stewardess picks up the radio mic and says her farewell to the passengers.

"Okay, everyone it's been a good flight. No, a great flight. No one fought anyone and I managed to keep my wig tight, this time around. I don't know your final destination once you depart from Philadelphia airport, but you can't stay here" she says with a smile. "This baby's only making this stop. No Baghdad, Iraq and definitely now Bin Laden visits to the underground tunnels will be requested. So please if you're trying to get that kind of tour, it ain't happening".

Everyone on the plane just sits motionless and shock by the flight attendant's comment. Was this supposed to have been a joke? From the looks of the passengers, the flight attendant was about to get a serious ghetto beat down right on the plane. (Go figure. Every plane ride has a ghetto person inside of them just waiting to bust out. But now? Bad business, just straight bad. *So unprofessional*).

CHAPTER 4

"Beep, Beep!" Sounds of car horns honking all around as people race to different taxis and limos, waiting outside of the airport.

"Come on grandma, I see an empty taxi". Rachel grabs their bags, walks over to the taxi and opens the door.

"Please take us to the train station. We have to catch the next train going to Trenton, before it pulls off". The cab driver begins to speak Spanish. Rachel does not understand a word he's saying.

"Excuse me sir, but I don't speak Spanish. Um… say… "No Espanola. Oh God. I knew I should have paid more attention in Spanish class".

The cab driver continues speaking in another language leaving Rachel and her grandmother confused, pissed off and now thinking they're going to miss the train as well.

"Sir look. Sir, please wait". Rachel tries again to explain to the driver what she wants. Seconds later a fine tall African-American man, dressed in a dark navy-blue suit, white shirt with a fashionable tie walks up to the cab and helps her out.

"Hello. Do you ladies need some help?"

"Yes, my grandmother and I need to get to the train station immediately, but this cab driver speaks Spanish and can't understand what I'm saying. I mean I don't speak Spanish and, well, you know, I'm just confused right now". He smiles at Rachel.

"Let me help you out, excuse me for a moment". He leans down to speak to the cab driver. "Favor de manejar estas damas a la esfacion del tren".

Rachel is surprised, yet impressed by what she has just witnessed. Not only was this man fine, he spoke fluent Spanish. The taxi driver smiles and then holds out his hand.

"Okay ladies, my work here is done. Now you have to pay the man" he says with a smile.

"Thank you so much" says Rachel as she throws her bags into the cab.

"Allow me to introduce myself. My name is Erwin Bowes, but my friends call me Pole". Rachel smiles as she places the last bag into the cab.

"Pole? Why Pole"

"As you can see, I'm as tall as a tree. A tree is very strong and can stand whatever weather that comes its way". The taxi driver blows the horn because he's ready to pull off.

"Well nice to meet you Mr. Bowes and thanks again." Pole reaches out for Rachel's hand. She cautiously holds out her hand as he leans in and place a light kiss on the back of her hand.

"Oh, believe me, the pleasure is all mines. By the way I did not get your name". Rachel tries to play hard ball, not giving off any signs of wanting to be more than just a friend to Mr. Nice Guy.

"No need. I doubt if I'll run into you again, take care, Pole".

Her grandmother is already in the cab with her seat belt on. The engine and pay-meter are running.

"Let's go Rachel. We're going to miss our train". Erwin Bowes (aka Pole) chuckles to himself. "And then again, you never know what the wind might blow your way, Mr. Black. So now you take care too. Ma' grandchild and I got to bounce".

The cab pulls off, head to the train station, and makes it in time for them to be on they're on their way home. After an hour and forty-five minutes have gone by, they finally pull into the Trenton train station. They grab their bags and head outside to see if they can jump into another cab and head home. A cab pulls up from the other side of the street. The driver gets out.

"Where you ladies going?".

"West Side, can ya' handle that playa?" says Grandma Agnes as she opens the door and puts her bags inside of the trunk.

CHAPTER 5

"The neighborhood still looks the same. Nothing really changed. Just about everybody's trying to get with somebody. Brothers, sisters and even some of the so-called church folks, are beginning to get loose. Back in the day people used to be discreet. Now they're wide open like a wild child jumping in the city water fountain, trying to get a token that somebody had thrown away".

Finally, the cab pulls in front of the house. They get out of the cab, pay the driver and go into the house. Her grandmother walks into the kitchen, turns on the light and pulls out a few pots and cooking utensils. She can hear Rachel talking to herself in the other room. She begins to recite a poem from the authoress Williams

"Wow grandma. Isn't that something? Someone at any given time will always try to steal someone's wish. They can also try to make it seem as if they created that very own dish. Just like that down home southern fried fish served with pork bacon, grits and scrambled eggs with cheese". Her grandmother stops what she's doing and says to herself

"Oh Lord, I don't know what she just said, but I hope she ain't on that stuff. She sounds a bit confused to me. And she didn't even rhyme".

Rachel walks over to the couch, take a seat and turn on the television. She hears her grandmother rattling pots and running the faucet water. She turns down the television to hear her grandmother talk.

"You'd be surprise to know how many people stop drinking whole milk and switched to 2% milk as if that's not gonna' make them constipated too". Her grandmother laughs. "And ya' know those unattended children are still running around in the streets late at night, while their momma's entertain their lovers or probably somebody else's husband. You see, they are always out there using their bang-bangs to get that dirty money to get their manicures and pedicures done, along with those tacky weaves. Oh dear, Rachel do you want something to eat?".

Rachel looks toward the kitchen. "Not right now". She stays put on the couch for a while and watch television. As she flips through the channel she sees a familiar show that watched when she was in college. It was called "Make Moves". The talk show was created by the author. She wrote the books "Relations Without Relationships: Real can hurt like a mutha" and "One Woman, Two Men and the Interference".

"Are you sure? I was just about to fix me a sandwich". Rachel gets up and walks into the kitchen to see what her grandmother is cooking.

"No grandma, that's fine. I'll grab something later"

"Are you sure? I have some pork chops, pig feet, pork grinds and pork bacon". Rachel frowns and grabs her stomach at the sound of pork.

"Yuk. Is there anything in that refrigerator that doesn't have a piece of pig attached to it?". Her grandmother looks at her and scratches her forehead.

"Huh. You say something, Ms. Rachel? Ya' momma grew up on pork". Rachel tries to clean up her comment.

"I said pig away grandma, it's your day". Her grandmother turns around to finish making herself a sandwich.

"Ha, ha, ha! Pork is good for the brain; you won't go insane. Ha, ha, ha!"

"No thanks grandma. Really, I think I'm going to grab a slice of pizza from the shop on the corner. I need to take a walk and get some air. Do you want me to bring you back a slice?"

"No. Do they have bacon bits? If so, get me a slice with extra PORK bits". Rachel leaves out of the kitchen. The smell of pork surfacing in the air starts to fill the room.

"Hey! Don't you want to see your room? I fixed it up for you". Rachel flops down on the couch and picks up the remote.

"Sure. I'll do that and then I'll go out". She decides to go upstairs to the room, open the door and walks in. She glances over the room, walks over to the window and opens the shade.

Her mind starts to wonder. She begins to get deep in thought and tries to remember what this room used to look like before her mother moved out.

"Being back in this room brings back a lot of memories. Well except for the changes that grandma had made. New curtains, a lighter color shade of paint and oh my God, a DVD player with surround sound? Boy lady, you sure out did yourself this time".

Rachel kneels down, looking closely at the DVD player. She notices a card taped to the side of the speaker. She opens the card and read. "*Rachel, I know this may not seem like much, but it's the least I could do. Now that you're out of college, I know you prefer the finer things in life. I just hope that this DVD player is a start. PS, make sure you don't forget to look in the closet. I got some of the hottest hits. Love you, grandma*".

Rachel's eyes begin to tear. "My grandmother is something. A DVD player is just what I wanted. Lord knows when I was in college, I only had a VHS player. Being high tech was never in the cards for me and neither was my cash flow. I bet I was the only person in the world that did not own a DVD". She walks over to the bedroom closet, opens it and grabs the case. She sees a Lauren Hill CD, Jesse J and Keisha Coles new joint.

"Okay, grandma got a little flavor. I love Lauren Hill. Ms. Hill is what they call her". She opens the package, places the CD inside the DVD and push play. The music begins… "It's funny how money change a situation, miscommunication leads to complications, your emancipation don't fit your equation…". She starts to dance like she's in a club full of people.

"Ho, hey, yeah, hey. Watch out, got it going on, step back before the brothas' catch a Jones. Can't you see, I'm too fly, see I can't lie, yeah, yeah".

Rachel slides over to the window still moving to the sounds of Lauren Hill. She looks out, slows down her groove and watches what's going on outside. Her grandmother comes up to the room, knocks on the door, and turns the knob to open the door. She sees Rachel standing over by the window. Her grandmother walks up behind her and place both of her hands-on Rachel's shoulders.

"Not much has changed since you've been gone"

"I know. It's almost sad to see that people who used to be on the right track, has now ended up on the wrong side". Her grandmother still standing behind her begins to wipe off a piece of lent off of Rachel's shirt.

"Now, now, you can't go round bad-mouthing folk, just cause you made up your mind to do what's right. People are struggling day in and day out, tryna' keep their lives together". Her grandmother starts to walk towards the bedroom door.

"I'm not bad-mouthing anyone. All I'm saying is that people can change. No one can force someone to take drugs, drink alcohol or force sexual advances on people, if they don't want to. Right?".

Her grandmother chuckles, turning the knob and opens the door.

"Rachel, baby. You're missing the point. There are a lot of peer pressure and extra inexcusable curricular activities going on out there". Her grandmother tries to inform her about facing reality (REALITY CHECK BOO).

"No. I don't think so grandma. You see I on the other hand turned out fine. Despite what happened to my mother, I still stayed strong, manage to finish college and now I'm preparing to find a great job"

"You turned out fine because you have a family that didn't want to see you become a statistic of this environment and be in a place that was not going to help you grow. Remember boo, we did that for you".

Rachel thinks to herself, "We? More like my mom". She turns around to face her grandmother. She picks up another CD and begins to listen to music while she changes her clothes.

"Rachel sometimes people don't have the same strength as you do. Some lost their family young to disease, war, tragic deaths and even to the system. It's hard out there".

Rachel pulls out her Alicia Keys CD. "Really, how hard is it just to say no?". Rachel begins to listen to the music.

"And you think it's just that easy to walk away from certain influences? Better yet, can you even imagine what demons are going through one's mind when they are in a situation and their backs are against the wall. Do you really have a clue?". Her grandmother stands in the doorway, watching and waiting for Rachel's response.

"No. But I do know that people have a choice. I did. I made it through"

Her grandmother chuckles again. "Yeah, you made it by the light mustache on your chinny chin-chin". The both of them laugh.

"You're real funny grandma. You got jokes"

"I keep em' poppin' like butter popcorn. Hey are you hungry or what? I've got some of my famous stew warming up on the stove".

Rachel turns around walks toward the window and closes the blinds.

"No thanks. I'm going to get a slice of pizza at the shop down the street. It's been a while since I had some real tomato sauce"

"Huh!" grandma says out loud with a laugh. "And you think the pizza man's sauce is homemade? Well, ya' better call Sam's Club. They'll tell you how many times the pizza man has been there. Since you got to run out now, dinner will be ready by 5pm. Don't be late". Her grandmother shuts the door and goes downstairs.

"Never. Your stew is like lightening. I don't want to be shocked for missing that". Her grandmother slides in a slick quote, finishing up Rachel's line.

"By the grace of God, if ya' miss, I'ma' strike ya' and hard".

"You're real funny grandma. How did you get to be so funny?"

"Like I said, I keep em' coming like the kids in the candy store, or the crack heads in the alley ways. Gotta fix? Trick?..."

Rachel starts to straighten her bags against the wall and hangs her clothes in the closet. "Okay. It's time for a shower, change these dress clothes and slip into something comfortable". Rachel takes off her clothes, grabs a house coat from the closet and put it on.

She picks up her suitcase, put it on the bed, opens it and pulls out a pair of bleached cut up jeans, a pair of panties and a black lace bra. "Now I need a shirt. I guess this old navy tank top will have to do for now. Okay, where's my Nike shox?" She reaches deep in her luggage and pulls out her sneakers. "I might as well get all the ware out of them I possibly can. Lord knows my toes need a break from those heels, pumps and open-toe sandals. You name it I wore it, and to all of the parties".

After Rachel finishes with her shower, she walks back into her room, turns on the radio and begins to get dress. The sweet sounds of the singer, songwriter, Alicia Keys plays over the airways. She wraps her own arms around herself and sings "I'm fallen, in and out of love with you…". She lotions herself down with cucumber melon lotion and sprays on her favorite perfume Cypher by Carol's

Daughter. After pampering herself she picks up her jeans and slides them on. "Oh boy, are these jeans getting tighter? Or am I getting thicker? Okay, now the shirt. Yeah, just lovely as ever".

Rachel checks her watch, grabs her jacket, ties it around her waist and heads out of the bedroom. She jogs down the stairs, looking for her grandmother.

"Grandma, grandma, where are you? Something smells good. It smells like baked chicken smothered in gravy with some good ole' homemade stuffing". Rachel gets to the bottom of the stairs and walk towards the kitchen. She hears Gospel music coming from the kitchen. It's Yolanda Adams "This Too Shall Pass". She opens the door and see her grandmother swaying from side to side, while washing the dishes.

Grandma Agnes loves her Gospel, her God and the fact that she has joy unspeakable joy. Her grandmother is flawless, unique and intelligent. She's the nicest person you will ever want to meet. Well at least that's what the meat produce man said after he tried to cheat Grandma Agnes out of a high price rump roast.

Rachel stands still trying not to interrupt, but she suddenly sneezes and her grandmother turns around.

"Well, well, did you change your mind? You want something to eat?"

"No. I just want you to know that I'm going out for a while. I'll be back later". Thoughts of being alone, comes across her grandmother's face, but she knows how young folks likes to be on the go. She takes the leftover food in the plastic containers out of the refrigerator and set it on top of the stove.

"Are you sure you're okay with me leaving? You know what, if it means that much to you, I'll just stay in and chill with you grandma". Grandma Agnes stands still with her back facing Rachel. The pots rattle and clank as she places them in the dishwasher.

"No dear. Please go on and enjoy the sun. You never know if you'll meet one of your old girlfriends, boyfriends, hood rats, you know, somebody. Just be careful".

Rachel smiles, kisses her grandmother on the cheek and heads towards the front door.

"Maybe". Her grandmother stops what she's doing and turns around to face her grand-daughter.

"Do you remember that girlfriend you used to hang out with back in high school?"

"Who? Molina Jacobs? Wow I haven't talked to her since I moved away from here"

"Yeah, she was, or is one of your best friends, right? No comment?". Rachel's eyebrows raise with a crooked grin.

"I'll see you later".

As she opens the door and walks out, she hears a horn blow at her. "BEEP BEEP!" Two guys in the car, with fitted baseball caps and white wife-beater t-shirts, were chilling and straight shooting the breeze while cruising down Rutherford Avenue. Loud conversation was coming across the street from some guys standing in front of an abandon house.

"Yeah, yeah. Here's forty for you shorty, I'll have the rest for you later on tonight and don't be late with my cake baby girl". Rachel steps off the porch and head down to the pizza shop. Little children from the neighborhood play hop-scotch and shoot hoops in the street as cars pass by, flying and ignoring the speeding limit.

Motor cycle riders and fancy cars slide through like they run the block. Believe it or not, they have been doing this since the neighborhood watch gave up due to a lack of support from the community, the leaders for a better society and even the man in charge of the city.

Deep down inside, Rachel feels there could be a change if everyone comes together and be the voice that the city needs to hear. Maybe? As she gets to the pizza shop, she opens the door and walk in. The smell of fresh pizza bakes in the 450-degree oven. Garlic knots and other flavors of pizza accent the round metal trays, and sits behind the glass. Italian music plays in the back while sounds of hip-hop plays from the outside. "Bang, bop-bop, Bang, bang bop-bop".

Young thugs and little mommas patrol the corners and bounce to the sounds of the most talented artist "50 Cent". "Hey, yeah! Get em' girl, throw that cash up, back that thang up". The fellas are off the chain and the block is changing day by day.

"Man! Money must be good. Young fellas on the street corners, still slinging rocks and snatching up all those young girl's assets. Yeah! Especially the ones that do not have a clue about what life is really all about" says Rachel (In her mind).

The worker walks from the back of the store, picks up a rag and sees Rachel patiently waiting to order.

"Hey ma' welcome to my pizza shop!". She smiles from his excitement.

"Hi. Can I have a slice with extra cheese and I'll have a chicken cheese steak with all the fixings. Thank you". The worker smiles as he takes Rachel's order.

"Wow, such mannerism from such a beautiful young lady. Where are you from? Not from around here I know, because you're too respectful. You show more respect than these hoodlums". Rachel doesn't look at the worker, she just sighs as she checks over the menu. One of the guys from the corner walks into the pizza shop with a bulk of cash in his hands and a black mild in his mouth.

"Yo! Ma' man. Give me a burger wit er' thang on it and a coke soda without ice". Rachel continues to look at the menu. "Yo! What's the special? I think I might want this chicken steak with extra mushrooms and cheese and that's it"

The worker becomes quite agitated and lashes out at the rude customer.

"Don't you see I have a customer here in front of you?" He goes off into the back and then returns with three different dishes for the special for the day. Rachel leans on the glass, opens up the menu and reads through it.

"What. You think you're the diamonds on a Tiffany bracelet? You think your temple is like gold?". Rachel ignores the brotha' as he tries to get next to her nerves, while watching her well defined curves. "A ma' you ain't all that".

Rachel continues to ignore the young thug. She waits for her food. "I'll also have a Pedrino Tuna sandwich with a side order of fries, cooked crispy please". She reaches in her jacket and pulls out a twenty-dollar bill and lays it on the counter. The brotha' looks at her twenty, sniffs like he's in for the kill and slowly approaches her.

She can see him coming from the corner of her eye and calmly places her hand on top of her twenty-dollar bill. She tries to act like she's looking at the desserts inside of the glass. He leans against the counter, pulls out another black mild and lights it. The weed smell floats in Rachel's direction. She quickly turns her head towards the entrance door and places her two fingers under her nose.

"Hey, hey! Put that out. I'm running a business here, you weed head!" says the owner coming from the kitchen area with Rachel's order. The brotha' takes a quick pull on the black mild, inhales with two quick breaths.

"Man look…this that good stank, ya' know" he says in a husky tone. "Ya' want some ma'?". He holds it out for Rachel to accept. "What's the matter? It ain't gonna bite you ma'"

"No thank you". She takes her food from the owner, hands him the twenty dollars and waits for her change. She heads out of the door and doesn't say a word. She can hear the brotha' creeping up behind her. He begins to shout out to her in a husky voice, puffing.

"Yo! You think you too good to take a hit? It might make ya' walk straight, with ya' stank booty". The pizza owner continues to look at Malik with disgust in his eyes. "Mmmm, I'm gonna keep my eyes on that, for real. See, she don't know she's already taken". Seconds later Eisha, an old neighborhood friend of Rachel's meets her at the coming out of the pizza shop.

"Hey girl, What's good? Your grandmother told me you were at the corner store. How does it feel to just breathe after those long four years of blood, sweat, tears and weak link brothas on campus?". Well girl, it feels great to me. Listen, my parents are away for the weekend and I got their condo all to myself. Let's celebrate, invite some dudes over and celebrate our accomplishments together. Maybe I'll let them stay over".

The thug looks on as Rachel walks down the street towards her grandmother's house. He yells out to Rachel "I'm gonna keep my eyes on you, for real! She don't know...I'm that dude...for real".

"Whatever" she says as she continues to walk away trying not to catch a contact from the scent of the weed. As Rachel gets closer to her grandmother's house her cell phone rings. She swaps her food bag from one arm to the other, reach in her jacket pocket and pull out her phone.

Rachel scrunches up her nose. "Yuck. You've just gotten from school and you're on a hoe stroll already?" Rachel laughs after she makes her comment.

"Whatever. I'm getting some tonight. It's been a while". Rachel clears her throat before she comments back. "And besides, I haven't seen him in a while. He's looking real good and he's got a little hustle on the side"

"Really"

"Oh, come on. Don't act like you're so perfect that you don't need a little act right yourself". Rachel gets closer to her front porch, opens the door and walks in.

"I've already gotten acquainted with Mr. Bad breath. He's okay, nothing too fly about him. He's kind of corny if you ask me".

"Girl, if you don't want him, I'll take a stab at it, okay boo. Shoot like Beyonce says you got to go wayyyyyy in the back of that closet and put on that freakum dress for your man. And then take it off Yeahhhhhha!".

Rachel continues to head towards the kitchen and preps herself to eat. There's a brief silence on the other end of the phone.

"Hello? Tramp? You still there" says Rachel and she takes a bite of her sandwich.

"Girl, I'm still here. I'm just trying to figure out what to put on so my man can take it off" she says to Rachel with a hard laugh.

"Oh, now he's your man. So,
I'm quite sure you'll be sharing tonight"

"Excuse me? I don't share"

"Oh? Did you kiss him?"

"Yes. When I was ten...and it was so good girl"

"Well. You just shared a kiss with approximately 200 other chicks from the block. Happy STDs trick" Rachel begins to laugh. "No. I'm just kidding, but seriously, just be careful and use a condom, okay."

"Wow, thanks mom" says her friend on the other line.

"By the way, make sure you tell him to get a blood test before you go low, low, low, low, low, low, low, low" Rachel says in a playful tone.

"Shut up! Ms. Goody-Two-Shoes. You really act like you're so perfect. I'm quite sure you've touched since you've been home. Come on. These brothas' got their hustle going on. Grab that dough before some scrubby chicken head comes along and take it".

"Look. I noticed a cute brotha but, he's all about the game. I promised myself I was not going to get off at the next exit just because it looks good. I'm patient. I can wait". Eisha looks at Rachel in a slick way,

"Who? Malik? Yeah, I saw the way he watched you". But she still needs to remember that Rachel's her girl, but she grew up. This is something Eisha can't get with...she never could and she never will.

"It's not that serious, he's alright"

Rachel's ready to end the conversation because her food is too good to waste.

"Yeah, okay whatever you say. Look it's nothing wrong with getting a little something on the side and still have it going on. It doesn't have to be serious, just give yourself a little play room to get ya' thang going on, still find you a banging job with your banging degree and then just blow em' off. Come on girl. Everybody's got an itch that needs to be scratched sometimes".

Rachel scratches her nose, picks up her drink and takes a sip. "Look I'll call you tomorrow". The door-bell rings and she get up to go to the door. She wonders who it could be. She looks out of the peep hole. "Oh God, I know this clown did not follow me home".

"What's up girl? You okay?".

"Let me go, I have an unexpected guest at the door". Her girlfriend smiles on the other end of the phone line.

"Yeah, okay. It must be time to get you some act right". Rachel hangs up the phone and opens the door. It's the dude from the pizza shop. Malik, the biggest drug dealer in the neighborhood. He's smart with his money, very handsome and he's definitely running things. He graduated from high school and took a few tech classes at DeVry, graduated but could not get a job because he was incarcerated as a juvenile. Yes. The system can pull rank if they want to. So, Malik made his money the only way he knew how. He survived on the streets and he has made a name for himself. He approaches Rachel's porch. Persistent and ready to claim his prize.

"You think I was gonna let you go that easy? Listen ma', grab your jacket and let's go for a ride". Rachel looks at him like he's lost mind for coming to her door.

"Look, I'm not interested, so go play with one of those hood rats on the corner. I have better things to do". He laughs at her and rubs his chin.

"I'm gonna get straight to the point. I like you. I like ya' slick talk. You got swagger ma', so come on let's take a ride and you can tell me all about yourself"

"No". He looks at her as if she's speaking another language. "No. I'm not interested".

"Hey, it's all good ma'. Like I said I see you and I'll be back. You'll make up your mind, have me over for some chips and whatever, I'll probably be talkin to ya' moms and all that other jive. You real pretty and I can see ya' smart. But don't be dumb. Holla at ya' boy. But later for now". He leaves off of the porch and Rachel shuts the door.

"He must be out of his mind. He has no clue of what to do with this right here".

She goes back to the couch, turns on the TV and looks at a movie. Seconds later the phone rings, it's her girl-friend's on the other line.

"Hey! Ms. Goody-Two-Shoes. You get any?"

"No. I'm not on that level of being wanted by the thug life". Rachel starts to laugh.

"Hey, you like Tupac, so what's the difference? Oh, you think you're too good to hang with a down to earth brotha?"

"No. I'm just not trying to be another one of those chicks who think that all they need is a quick weave and a couple of dollars in their pockets to make them feel like they're at the top of the food chain". Her friend begins to feel some kind of way.

"Oh, so you think I'm one of those chicks just because I didn't go to some big-name college like you. I got goals too". Rachel tries to take control of the conversation.

"What are you talking about? Your college was I guess okay…" Eisha lashes back out to Rachel in a bitter tone.

"Yeah! But you went all the way down South. I was at the borderline". Eisha's voice begins to tremble as she listens to Rachel.

"I'm not saying that. Okay, he's cute, but I don't know. It's just that I'm better than that and I think I deserve better. Not a thug".

"Wow"

"Wow what?"

"Rachel you think you're too good to get got. We let me tell you something baby girl, like I said everybody's got an itch. So, you better get with the program because this money out here ain't gone last long. So jump on that brotha' before some other chick do. Or are you too good for that? I've got my degree, so what. But I'm damn sure gonna do me, regardless. As long I know when enough is enough and when to quit. Shoot I'm good for now." Eisha prepares for her grand exit out. "Oh, would you look at the time. I got to go. My boo is giving me a few dollars, so I can get my weave done. And boo-boo I don't need to feel like I'm on top of the food chain, because I already run it. Later. Wait, I got a present for you." Eisha gets up from the couch, reaches in her purse, pulls out a note and passes Rachel. Eisha heads out the front door and makes her way back towards the end of the street to meet Malik. He passes her some cash.

"Did you give it to her?"

"hmmm, I sure did. Like I said, everybody's got an ITCH".

Malik makes a quick run back home to check on his mother. He enters the house. The lights are dim and he walk towards the kitchen. He hears some music coming and walks through the door. He sees his mother cooking on the stove. The smell is out of this world. She turns around and smiles.

"Where have you been young man. You know I don't like you walking in those streets all times of night. It's getting dangerous out there boy". Malik goes over to his mother and kisses her on the check.

"Come on mom. I'm a grown man and I have my own car"

"Yea. Thank God for your father for finally coming through on something". Malik turns up his lip.

"Please don't talk about that dead-beat dad. He hasn't done anything for me". His mother cuts him off.

"Now you stop that kind of talk! He's still your father. I know he hasn't been there much but when we need something he comes through". Malik sucks his teeth and states a sarcastic comment.

"Yea…I bet he did come…through, dirty rat". His mother slashes out. This time with force.

"I told you to watch your mouth and I mean it. I didn't raise you to be that way!". Suddenly there's a knock at the door. "KNOCK KNOCK".

"Hey I thought I heard you two in here. What's for dinner?"

"So, this bum is letting himself in our home now…I'm out!". Malik leaves out of the kitchen aggressively brushing past his father.

"I told you one day I'm gonna sit his but down…I still pay the bills around here"

"Larry, he's angry because you never took time with him. He's a young man now. You didn't handle that right at all"

Larry looks at her with disgust and shakes his head.

"Well, if you would have been a better woman to me, maybe I would have stayed home more" He goes over to the cabinet reaches for a glass and the bottle of scotch.

"Oh, really? I guess that explains why you slept with Trina for all those years. Wasn't I enough for you?" Before she could finish her sentence, Larry puts has his hands around her throat.

"Don't ever say that woman's name again! She's done, no more talk of her and I mean it! And don't ever mention a thing to Malik. He's already a live wire" He takes his hands from her throat.

"Why? Am I going to end up just like her? In the gutter, dead?" Larry puts his glass down and this time gets back up in Malik's mother's face.

"I told you not to say a word. You tryna' get me locked up. I'm a lawyer…and I worked too hard for that. Now get my dinner and get your ass up-stairs. I need my time and then I'm out of here". She stares at Larry and then does what he say to do.

He gets his plate and goes to the bedroom.

"At times like this I wished I killed his ass myself. But we've done too much to turn back now. And Tina's death is something we have to take to the grave".

Later that night Rachel lays on her bed looking over old photos of her mother, father and old neighborhood. She thinks about what her childhood was like and the places that her mother took her. Her mother told her so many times that she loved her that she would do everything in her power to keep her safe. Time has passed and Rachel's all grown up. Life begins, but what would be in store for her from here on out is another question.

She closes the photo album, puts on her ear plugs and begins listening to tunes on Pandora. Music takes you to another place when you're feeling sad, happy, confused or even angry. Her favorite song comes on by Alessia Cara "Here". The lyrics sets in her mind, intertwining and thoughts of getting away from the very place that she thought was safe, now haunts her. Her friends from the block changed and she now wonders how she is going to deal with the pressures of others wanting her to be like them; all about the streets and not about building a strong foundation, having a career and living life to the fullest, just like she promised her mother she would do.

She looks over towards the night stand next to her bed and sees the note folded with the phone number on it. She gazes for a few moments thinking to herself; "What does this thug want with my life. He has nothing to offer me". She stares at it a few more times.

"Rachel! Are you okay, do you want some warm milk baby?" says her grandmother from the other room.

"Uh, no, I'm, I'm okay. Good night". She turns to look at the note again. This time she takes it off the night stand, opens it. "Well, it probably wouldn't hurt just to call…I mean…I'm not trying the marry the thug".

My how tables suddenly turn and now things are put in motion. Rachel waits a few more minutes before she makes the call. She picks up her cell phone and dials Malik. As the call rings on the other line Malik sees that it's Rachel's cell because Eisha had already prepared him with the 7-digits. While Malik sits alone in the park waiting on his next drop the Security officer walks up to him pulls out his flash light and flashes Malik right in his eyes. Malik doesn't even flinch.

"You know I'm used to this by now, right? Aren't you pass your bed time crooked officer" Malik says in a sarcastic manner? He knows this officer too well.

"What you doing out here youngster. It's late and your pass your curfew". The officer begins to search through his pockets

"Yeah, ya' pockets looking kind of fat. What you got in there?" Malik stands up and assumes the position.

"Skittles, doughnut boy". The Security officer grabs Malik by the collar of his jacket and yokes him up.

"You think you're smart! Think you can't get caught. You don't know who you're messing with!". Another officer rolls up on the officer ruffing up Malik and gets out of the car.

"Yo! Easy, let him go. He's small time we just need him to tell us where's the big dealers are. That's all". The officer turns to Malik and acts as if he's really being the good guy. "As you can see, I have to be my brother's keeper. Now what are you doing out so late?". Malik fixes up his clothes and sits back on the bench, sizing both of the officers up and plans for a get-
away, if things look like it's about to go bad.

"I'm waiting for my girl. It's her birthday and I'm late getting her the gift I got from Tiffany's". The officers begin to laugh.

"Be for real…I see your type all the time. Bling, Bling all over the place. Grills

just shining like a bright Christmas tree".
Malik continues to look at their body

language, making sure that their hands don't go somewhere it really doesn't need to go.

"Let's go, he ain't worth it. Yo' get outta here. Find something constructive to do besides hanging on the street corners" says the officers proceed to back to their patrol cars.

"Why thank you officer for your kind words of wisdom. I will do just that". Malik salutes them as they walk off. His cell phone rings. "Talk to me". He answers as he continues to walk back
to the block.

"Hey it's me. Rachel. Um so what you doing?".

"Nothing, What's up?" Malik now sounding uninterested in what Rachel has to say.

"You. I want to know if you want to go out and talk" her voice sounding a bit shaky but she gets up the nerve to stay on the phone.

"That's it? Just talk? Look Rachel I'm going to keep it absolutely real with you.

You are the finest and smartest thing I've seen walking this planet Boo. But it's no rush if you're not feeling me. I'll call you tomorrow. If I'm available". He hangs up the phone.

"Malik?!?!" She looks at the phone in unbelief.... dead tone. "Hello? Hello Malik? I knew it. I knew I should not have called him. Now I'm looking like boo-boo the fool, okay girl just chill, get your mind right. It ain't that serious, right, yeah yeah that's right, not that serious. Yo' I'm tripping. Forget his bald-head, rat-a-tat-tat looking butt". She begins to put her music back on.

Malik waits a few minutes, counts to five "1, 2, 3, 4, 5" Then he calls her back. She sees the call coming in from the flashing light on her cell phone. She jumps up and down, does the cabbage, and the duggy. Finally, she clears her throat and answers the phone, sounding as if she's tired and uninterested.

"Hello...What do you want"

"Hey meet me out front and go get something to eat. You hungry?"

"Yeah, yeah food sound good I'm on my way". She grabs her jacket and goes downstairs to meet Malik. She opens the door and there he is, standing on the porch with his back facing the door.

"Ready?"

"Yes" she says in a calm voice.

"Good because what I have to say, do and show you is gonna take time. So, I really hope you are ready". She steps off the porch now sizing him up from the top of his head to the bottom of his feet.

"Lord this man is fine and he's bow-legged too. Lord help me with this one. Hold me Lord". She stays out with Malik until the sun comes up and tries to creep back in before her grandmother notices she's gone. But that's not always the case.

Grandma Agnes is already up, and in the kitchen getting ready to prepare breakfast. Food is sizzling and smelling right…just like the good ole days when her mother used to cook breakfast and sing at the same time.

"Oh, it's a beautiful morning and I feel good. She sets plates for breakfast. "Rachel! Rachel! Come on down and get some breakfast I got turkey bacon, turkey sausage, turkey links, turkey patties, cheese eggs and buttered grits with wheat toast". Rachel comes into the kitchen already dressed and ready so, so early on a Saturday morning.

"Oh, wow, everything looks great…oh grandma you really out did yourself. But you know…I already have a breakfast date waiting for me, love you". She goes to kiss her grandmother on the cheek.

"So how was it, staying out late and spending all of your time with Malik. I hope you protected your goodies my dear". Her grandmother begins to prep the table for breakfast.

"How do you know it was Malik I was out with?" she says sounding suspicious"

"The streets talk. I maybe old but I not dumb. I hear everything that goes on. I'm surprised".

"Surprised? I'm just going to breakfast. It's not like we're running off to get married" Rachel giggles to herself trying to play off the conversation.

"So, I see you finally got the

ITCH" "Grandma come on". Her grandmother cuts her off.

"That's the type of itch ya' momma had when she messed with that crazy man that took her life straight to the gutter, Hell is the real word for it".

"So, you think that's something I want to remember. That thing ways on me over and over again. I'm nothing like her". Her grandmother puts down her fork and walks towards her and touches her face.

"Rachel baby, you are everything like her, so just be careful. You said yourself that you were better than that, right? Rachel begins to get teary eyed.

"Enjoy your turkey bacon grandma. Just like you said yourself, everybody's entitled to change". Rachel leaves back out of the house and sees Malik talking to a man. She waits on the porch and looks from a distance. Then she decides to walk towards them.

"Hey Malik, did I catch you at a bad time?"

"No. He was just about to make his grand exit". The man steps in on the conversation between Malik and Rachel.

"My, my, my so this is your friend. Your mother told me someone was taking up your time, got you on the straight path and slowing down from being in the streets like you used to be" He looks at Rachel as if he's seen her somewhere before.

"She just a friend…But, if you would have done your job, you would have had some of my time too, but you lost that privilege years ago"

"Mmm, okay, I deserve that". Larry looks at Rachel again. 'You look like someone I used to know, a long-time age. Tina? Right?" Rachel looks stunned

"You don't know her. Don't you got a plane to catch?" Larry prepares to walk off, but Rachel speaks up right before he leaves

"Yes". Larry turns around. "My mother's name was Tina. Did you know her well?"

"You know what, my mistake, I thought you just looked familiar. You know what, come to think of it, it was someone else. They say everyone has a twin out there somewhere. Look Malik it was real good seeing you again. I'll catch you later. Oh, and it was truly a pleasure seeing you". Larry walks off to get back in his car, but looks back one more time at Rachel. "Yes, truly a pleasure to see you, again".

Malik and Rachel walk off in the direction towards her grandmother's house. She looks at him as if she wants to ask him questions about the man he was talking to. The chill she felt hearing her mother's name made her want to question what the man knew about her mother, but didn't want to cause any waves because she did not know the man. But if he's throwing out scenarios and then trying to act as if it's nothing, then it definitely a question she needs to ask.

Malik tries to get her attention, pulls her arm to stop and ask her for a favor.

"Look before we get close to your house can I leave my bag at your there?" She looks down at the dark backpack and frowns a bit.

"No. I don't know if you're trying to have me hold something illegal. Besides, I don't even know you that well"

"If it makes you feel better here go ahead and look" Malik holds the back pack up to Rachel's face and she looks without hesitation.

"Malik these are diplomas and certificates of accomplishments you've done…But why are they in a bag? Aren't you proud of what you've done? What you are capable of doing? With the right people in your corner and positive energy, you can get to that place where you really want to be?" She smiles, but Malik is not moved by her excitement

"You think it's that easy to get a good paying job once you finish college? Do you?

"Well, I'm looking, but it'll happen if you just be more persistent. Just get that motivation and drive to make moves baby" She puts her arms around him and look him in his eyes.

"Oh, now I'm your baby. Just a minute ago I was the thug who loved his game"

"Nah…I'm just looking out for a brotha'". She pushes him away acting as if she's not feeling him.

"Look Rachel, the corporate world sees what they only want to see. I went on a lot of interviews, I prepared myself and well, cut my hair, wore the suit and tie, the whole nine" Malik removes hit snap back cap and scratches his head.

"So, you're just going to give up?"

"No. I'm just pacing myself nothing big". They make it back to Rachel's house and take a seat on the bench. He reaches into his pocket and pulls something out.

"What's this?". Malik places a small piece of candy in her hand.

"Breakfast"

"A Hershey's kiss? I think my grandmother makes still makes breakfast better than anyone on the planet" They both begin to laugh.

"Yeah, I figure since this is the closest, I'm going to get to touching your lips I thought it not robbery to do it this way. I can't go wrong. Right?" Rachel punches him in the arm, takes the h

Hershey's kiss and then kisses him on the cheek. Malik feels like he's on top of the world. But for how long. To him being in Rachel's presence was too good to be true.

"You know we can build this foundation together college boy" She laughs and rocks against his shoulder and he rocks her right back.

"Go head, now you know a brotha' got the educational capacity to take life to another level, now you wanna be all up on me. Wow I practically had to stalk you to get you to just sit with me really, really Rachel". They laugh and get up from the porch.

"Shut up. You a'ight. You ain't all that". Suddenly two guys run up on them with guns. Their faces were covered with bandanas and forced the Malik and Rachel to lie on the ground. Rachel was shaken and nearly pees on herself. Malik stands his ground. He was not going down without a fight. Rachel begs Malik to get down. But protecting what he has matters to him the most.

"Give me ya' money and ya' bling!"

"Get down, face down now!"

Rachel falls to the ground, but Malik tries to fight one of the guys and pulls off his skull cap. The dealer steps back and has his gun aimed at Malik. Malik knows these stick-up kids.

"Meechi? Are you serious! what…what are you doing man?" Malik says while out of breath. The other gun-man screams out to his partner in crime.

"C'mon dude we ain't time for this! Do it! Do it now!". Meechi hesitates for a minute because he knows that it's going to be hell to pay after this goes down, but the peer pressure is a mutha when one is on the other end of the gun.

"Yeah. I'm very serious (BANG, BANG!!! Two shots fire out and Malik falls, the two guys run off Rachel runs to his side screaming, lifts him on her as far as she can and holding him in her arms. She cradles him the same way she cradled her mother 14 years ago. The stick-up clan runs to the end of the block runs around the corner and meets up with Larry. By-standers look on while neighbors come out of their homes. They see Rachel with blood on her and Malik looking lifeless in her arms. She continues to yell out for help.

"Help!!! Please somebody call the cops, ambulance someone please!!!". The shooters toss the guns in Larry's trunk and get rid of the masks and waits for their pay that Larry promised them.

Larry claps his hands as if he just seen an amazing, yet chilling show that the world will talk about for years…even when he's gone.

"Did you do it? I told you those dealers had the cash to pay you back"

"It was Malik. I shot Malik" He begins to shake, wiping the sweat off his forehead.

"What? What are you talking about!" Larry grabs his head and begins to go for the thug's throat with his bare hands. He throws him to the ground, pulls out a pistol from his side and puts it to the thug's head.

"I swear I didn't know he was going to be there, but you told me to take him out!!!". Larry gets him up off the ground, he breaks away and takes off running. Larry jumps in his car and takes off.

"Oh God, what have I done?" Larry coasts to the scene and sees Rachel by Malik's side with the ambulance placing him on the stretcher and puts him in the van. Rachel climbs in behind them. Her grandmother comes out of the house and yells to her.

"Rachel!!!"

Rachel's eyes are closed and she's rocking back and forth. She's holding Malik's hand.

"Please, please help me, he's changed, doesn't that count for something

Lord. I know he's not perfect, but please, please let him live". Her grandmother approaches the van trying to get Rachel to listen.

"My child, what makes you so sure he's changed? God doesn't make mistakes. Come home. Please don't go down that same path like your mother, Please Rachel!!! Get out of the van!!!". The paramedics guides her grandmother away from the van.

"Ma'am we have to go! We have to go now or we'll lose him". She backs away and watches Rachel as she still holds onto his hand.

"Please, I'll pray for his life to be spared. Take me please! Take me!". Her grandmother backs up further as the ambulance's doors shut. The workers jump in the van and pulls off. The neighbors all stand in the street and shake their heads. The cop's gestures for the streets to clear so no one interferes with the yellow tape. Larry pulls off and tries to get his thoughts together.

Rachel's grandmother walks off but words of wisdom seeps from her lips as she walks pass the pool of blood on her front porch.

"My child, that call is up to God. I'm not telling you not to pray, but whatever you do you better do it now. You better know that God is a jealous God.

Rachel continues to pray for Malik as one of the paramedics works diligently to stop the bleeding.

"Ok, ok God please give Malik another chance, he's trying to do better, he's trying to be a man now Lord, please, please hear me, please". As they pull up to the emergency room the paramedics jump out, run to the back of the van, opens it and lets Rachel out first then the stretcher follows. They quickly roll Malik into the ER. Rachel waits in the waiting room and sees Larry seconds later coming in behind them. Rachel grabs Malik's bag close to her as Larry walks closer towards her.

"Rachel? I heard about Malik. Where is he now?" Larry says as he keeps a close eye on the bag that Rachel has in her hands. Rachel stares at him, this time, really taking a good look at him. She feels on the bag and this time notice that something was overlooked. Malik has a weapon in the bag. She reaches in, but doesn't pull it out. She gives Larry a hard stare and feels some uneasiness towards him. She can't quite put her finger on it. But she knows something is not right with Larry.

"You said I looked familiar to you. You said my mother's name. How do you know my mother?"

"Look Rachel, I know you're scared right now, but I need to know where Malik is. Look we can go together". Larry tries to get closer to her but this time she puts her hand completely on the gun in Malik's bag but does not pull it out yet. Larry starts to get agitated but tries to keep his cool.

"How well do you know my mother! You said her name! You said Trina!"

"Look I don't know I was just rambling on, I don't know your mother, or maybe I do. I know a lot of women baby". Larry tries to get Rachel to calm down because the people in the hospital were starting to take notice of Rachel's hostile actions towards Larry.

"My mother's name was Tina. She was shot and killed when I was 14 years old. She loved you so much and took so much from you that you took her away from me. She was all I had and you took her from me!!! Rachel begins to cry still holding the bag with the gun in it. This time she has her finger on the trigger. Larry tries to fast-talk her. But this time Rachel pulls the gun out on him. He's not afraid but knows that someone's going down and it's not going to be him.

People in the hospital start to move out of the way. The nursing staff calls for help and Rachel has a clear shot of the man who took her mother from her.

"If you shoot me, you'll lose Malik. He cares about you and I know how you feel about my son".

"Your son? Malik is your son?" Rachel is in shock.

"Yes. He didn't tell you?" Security Yells out again to Rachel.

"Rachel you're a smart girl. Don't be stupid like your mother. She was weak, naïve, huh, all beauty and no brains. The more I think about it maybe she did deserve to die. I did everything for her but she just wanted more and I couldn't give her that. My wife and Malik needed me more."

Rachel breaks down in tears falling to her knees. She takes her focus off Larry and slowly lowers the gun. As the cops finally arrives, they see Larry pulling out his gun from his side and aim it at Rachel's head ready to pull the trigger. The cops go into action, and takes Larry out with two shots

"No!" (BANG, BANG!!). Larry falls to the ground. Rachel looks up at the security officer holds up her hands and stay still. They see another gun next to Rachel and was ready to take a shot. The Nurse from the front desk heard everything and yelled for the cops not to shoot

"She's innocent. That man just confessed to killing her mother. It's his gun officer! Please don't shoot!!!". The cops slowly approach Rachel, lean down and picks up the gun. She continues to shake as the nurse runs over to her aid and covers her with a blanket and takes her to a secure room. The officers then close off the area with yellow tape, and get Larry to the ER.

"He's still breathing" says one officer as he checks his pulse. Get a doctor to check his progress, get two officers on his door when he comes out of ER and when this bastard recovers he's going to jail. We've been looking for him for a long time".

Six months has passed and Rachel has been at the hospital visiting Malik, helping him with therapy. As he was recovering, Rachel helps tutor him to get him ready for college. The day finally comes when Malik would be released, and start his life all over again.

"Oh, where's my manners? Come on slow poke, the doctor said you need all the exercise you can get. And soon you will be back to your new self". Malik uses a cane to move to help him move around. The doctor insists he moves slow the first few days and stay up on his therapy.

"I'm coming. Man, you are tough, but it's cool. I still love you"

"Love? Wow that's a word I haven't heard in a long time. And you know what it finally feels good. Often times we worry about how our lives are going to turn out, are we going to have that special someone there to keep us from harm?" says Rachel smiling.

"And sometimes we put ourselves in harm's way. In all reality we cannot change our mindset unless we change our situation, and the environment we live in".

Life, so delicate, so precious and so easy to take away, when you're not careful. Rachel and Malik both learned that nothing in life is free, and those who have something real should never take advantage of it.

Made in the USA
Middletown, DE
05 October 2022

11696062R00085